Blender 3.6

The beginner's guide

Allan Brito

Description and data

Technical info about the book

Author: Allan Brito

Edition: 4th (Revision 5)

Cover image credits: Allan Brito

Blender version used in the Book: 3.6

ISBN: 9798858779582

First edition date: August 2023

Imprint: Independently published

Editing and design: Allan Brito

Help and support:

https://www.blender3darchitect.com/contact/

About the author

Allan Brito is a Brazilian architect who is deeply passionate about integrating open-source technology into design and architectural visualization. With a rich history of exploring various open-source tools since 2005, Allan has broadened his focus beyond Blender to encompass a wide range of open-source software utilized in architecture and design. One of his core objectives is to support artists across these fields by guiding them in leveraging open-source tools to their advantage.

For insights on the extensive use of open-source software in architecture and design, visit blender3darchitect.com. Though the site began as a hub for Blender users, it has evolved to cover a plethora of open-source software. Allan continues to share articles daily, providing valuable information and resources to the open-source design community.

Who should read this book?

The primary objective of this book is to give any aspiring or experienced digital artist a fast way to start using Blender 3.6 with confidence. From simple concepts like user interface manipulation to more advanced topics such as light and rendering. We will start from the very beginning, covering critical steps required to get you comfortable with Blender. If you are planning to create 3D models, animations, and overall rendering, this book will help you start from scratch.

By the end of this book, you will have a solid knowledge of how Blender 3.6 works and what it takes to create digital content.

You don't need any previous experience with Blender to follow the chapters.

Foreword

Welcome to the world of Blender—a robust tool designed for every facet of digital art creation. Its utility spans across sectors such as animation, design, gaming, and architecture. Simply put, Blender is your go-to if it's the digital creation you're after.

Remember the buzz when version 2.8 rolled out? The spike in Blender's popularity wasn't mere coincidence. Enhanced user experiences meshed with groundbreaking features, and Eevee's real-time rendering emerged as the star, offering swift and transformative render capabilities. But Blender's innovation journey is ongoing, with new enhancements unfolding quarterly.

Our mission with The Beginner's Guide to Blender 3.6 is straightforward: demystify Blender for the budding artist or the curious aspirant. Commencing with the interface basics, we progressively touch upon areas like 3D modeling, animation, and rendering. And if you're looking to shift from older Blender versions, this guide promises a smooth transition.

Embrace the journey, absorb the wisdom, and by the end, let Blender be an integral part of your creative toolkit!

Allan Brito

Downloading Blender

One of the most significant advantages of Blender when comparing to similar tools is their open-source nature. You can use Blender without any hidden costs or subscriptions! All you have to do is download Blender and start using it. How to download? To download Blender, you should visit the *Blender Foundation* website:

```
https://www.blender.org/download/
```

Another option is to get a development version, which has the most up to date tools and features:

```
https://builder.blender.org
```

The development versions offer a peek of upcoming releases as *alpha* and *beta* versions. They feature new tools and options, but may also have bugs and instabilities. You should not use them for critical projects. For this book, we will use version *3.6 of Blender*, but the vast majority of techniques will still work with later versions.

Using the following address gives you access to the entire release history of Blender:

```
https://download.blender.org/release/
```

In the release history, it is possible to get current and old versions of Blender. For instance, you can download Blender 1.0! What version should you download? Get the latest stable release from the Blender Foundation website; it is the safest option. Use the first link from this section.

Download book files

You can download the Blender files used in the book in the following address:

```
https://www.blender3darchitect.com/b36beginners
```

All files use Blender 2.83, 2.9, 3.2, or 3.6. The ZIP file will include:

- Base files
- Textures
- HDR maps
- 3D Models

Intentionally left blank

Chapter 1 - Blender user interface and 3D Navigation

Embarking on the first chapter of "Blender 3.6: The Beginner's Guide", we are set to unravel the intricacies of Blender's core features and lay the foundation stone for your proficiency.

Imagine this chapter as your compass, steering you through Blender's multifaceted landscape. As a traveler would rely on a map to traverse unknown terrains, consider our "terrain" to be Blender's multifarious user interface.

Once we've laid the groundwork for the user interface, the spotlight will shift to another cardinal component of Blender: the Editors. These specialized compartments hold the tools that define Blender's capabilities. Together, we'll navigate through the process of choosing and toggling between these Editors. Furthermore, you'll learn the art of designing your Editor layouts and safeguarding them as Workspaces.

At this early juncture in your Blender odyssey, we'll illuminate the concept of the active Editor and its associated shortcuts. Recognizing that the active Editor determines the operational sphere of a shortcut is pivotal. As we dive into the rich pool of tailored shortcuts for varied operations, our primary emphasis will be on 3D Navigation.

Rounding off this chapter, we'll discuss object selection techniques and unveil Blender's ace in the hole: the 3D Cursor. Mastering this tool will empower you to exert precise control over object placements and alterations.

Here is a list of what you will learn:

- Navigating the Blender interface, including splitting and managing editors and using Workspaces

- Saving your projects and managing content efficiently

- Understanding and using the active Editor and shortcuts

- Mastering the essentials of 3D navigation and zoom controls

- Maneuvering the 3D Cursor for precise object placement and manipulation

1.1 First time with Blender

After the installation process, you will open the software and see a quick setup screen asking how would you like to use Blender. The most crucial choice you have to make on this screen is how you want to handle object selection. The screen only appears when opening Blender for the first time.

In the past, Blender used the *right mouse button* to select objects, which is the opposite of all other graphical applications. Starting in Blender 2.8, the new default behavior is to use the *left mouse button* for selection.

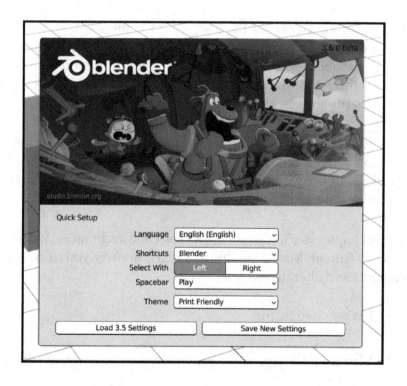

Figure 1.1 - *Blender Quick Setup*

In the *Quick Setup*, you can confirm the *Select With Left* and keep all other options in their default settings. One of the reasons to change the selection settings is for artists migrating from older versions of Blender. You can also change the Shortcuts template.

For the rest of the book, I will assume you choose the "Left" option (*Select With*) from the Quick Setup (Figure 1.1).

What if you have to make changes to those settings later? You can review them using the **Edit → Preferences...** menu. To modify your selection button, use the *Keymap* tab in the preferences to swap between the left or right mouse buttons for selection (Figure 1.2).

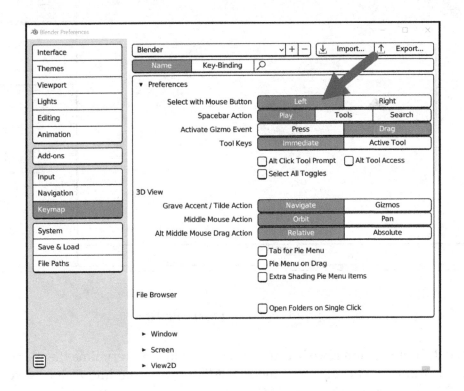

Figure 1.2 - *User preferences*

Why is that so important? Because some additional options regarding the user interface work based on the current selection settings. For instance, we won't have the *Context Menu* if you choose the *right-button* for selection. The Context Menu has many options and tools for the general management of 3D objects, which we will use a lot during the book.

You will see the Blender user interface after setting all options with the Quick Setup. At first, it may look intimidating for artists migrating from other graphical applications, but you will become familiar with time and practice.

Info: At the Quick Setup, you will also have the option to pick a theme for your Blender User Interface. The default theme is "Blender Dark." I use the "Print Friendly" for the book to ensure that all screenshots are clearly visible. You can change the theme at any time using the Edit → Preferences... menu and go to the Theme tab.

In Figure 1.3, you can see the default user interface of Blender.

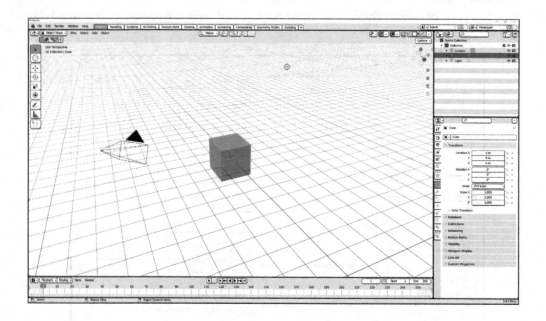

Figure 1.3 - Default user interface

That is the default user interface because it is what you see every time Blender starts after a fresh install. You can rearrange and modify Editors from the interface in several ways. What is an Editor? Each division in the interface is an Editor that handles a particular type of data. In Blender, we have lots of different specialized Editors and during a project development, we have to use multiple Editors at the same time.

For instance, you will find the extensive Editor at the center with a single cube, camera, and light as the *3D Viewport*. That is the Editor responsible for displaying 3D data and will allow you to manipulate 3D models. You can work with 3D modeling and visualize your projects in a tridimensional space in this Editor.

Here are other essential Editors in Blender:

– **Properties Editor**: Shows options regarding the selected object to edit and change properties like materials, modifiers, and more.

- **Outliner**: List all objects in a scene and also give access to collections of objects. You can also rename and control the visualization of objects.

- **Timeline**: Gives you a quick way to control animation data to add and set frames and keyframes.

Within each Editor, you'll notice a horizontal bar known as the header. This header showcases various menus and controls specific to that Editor. One prominent feature of the header is the Editor selector, typically located on the left side of the bar. By selecting this option, you can seamlessly switch the current Editor to any other available in the drop-down list (Figure 1.4)

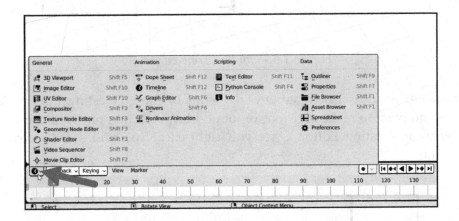

Figure 1.4 - Editor selector

That is useful when you want to quickly access tools available at a particular Editor in Blender without creating new interface divisions.

Tip: Every Editor has a horizontal header that displays additional menus and options. It is usually at the top of each Editor. You can flip their position to the top or bottom by right-clicking at the header and choosing Flip to Bottom or Top.

1.1.1 Splitting and managing editors

To customize the user interface for your needs, you can resize and modify the divisions for each Editor. To resize an Editor, place your mouse cursor at the border of an existing Editor. Once the Cursor turns to a double arrow, you can click and drag to resize (Figure 1.5).

17

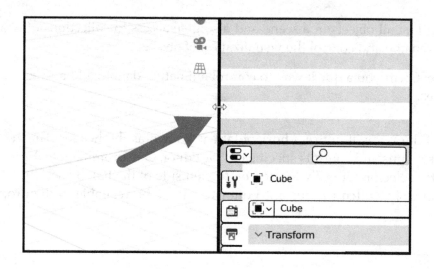

Figure 1.5 - *Double arrow cursor*

Besides resizing, we can also create new divisions or merge existing Editors. You have two options if you want to make divisions or join Editors. The first one is to use a right-click at the border of an existing Editor. Once you right-click, you will see the Area Options menu (Figure 1.6).

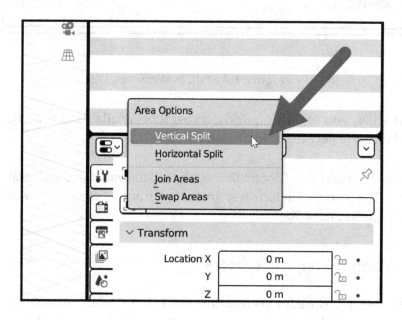

Figure 1.6 - *Area Options*

There you will find:

- **Vertical Split**: Creates a vertical division at your current Editor.

- **Horizontal Split**: Creates a horizontal division at your current Editor.- **Join Areas**: Join two editors with the same border.

- **Swap Areas**: You can swap between the two Editors sharing the border where you right-clicked.

Once you start the joining process, your mouse cursor turns into a small arrow, allowing you to choose which Editor expands. Once an Editor expands and take the space of an existing division, you have single Editor on that space. Removing an Editor from the interface doesn't affect 3D data (Figure 1.7).

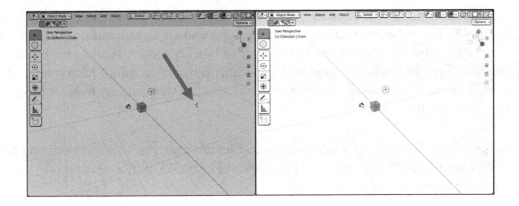

Figure 1.7 - *Expansion arrow*

The second option to manage Editors and divisions is to place your mouse cursor in the corner of any existing division. Once your cursor hovers over a corner, it will change into a small cross. The cross gives you the option to start a process of splitting or joining Editor.

Here is how it works:

- **Splitting:** Click and hold the left mouse button, and move the cursor horizontally or vertically. You will get a division using the opposite direction in which you move the mouse cursor. For instance, if you move up or down (vertical), your new division will be horizontal.

– **Joining:** After clicking and holding the left mouse button, move the cursor toward an existing Editor, and Blender will try to merge the current Editor with the one you are targeting. Depending on how you want to join those Editors, choose a corner that makes it easier to target another Editor. Pick a corner close to the Editor that you want to interact.

Knowing how to handle Editors and divisions is essential to keep you productive in Blender.

*Tip: You can also use the **View → Area → Duplicate Area into New Window** to detach an Editor from the interface. That is useful for moving Editors between multiple monitors.*

1.1.2 Using Workspaces

As you spend more time with Blender, you'll naturally develop personalized layouts, organizing Editors in ways that best suit specific tasks or projects. To streamline your workflow in future projects, Blender offers a feature known as Workspaces. A Workspace is a tailored arrangement of Editors, each designed with a distinct purpose in mind. Moreover, not only can you create your own custom Workspaces, but you can also import these settings from an existing Blender file.

Several pre-made Workspaces are available in Blender that you can choose using the selector at the top of your 3D Viewport. If you look at Figure 1.3, notice several tabs at the interface top with names such as:

– Layout

– Modeling

– Sculpting

– UV Editing

The default user interface of Blender is a Workspace with the name of *Layout*. That is the first tab on the left. Workspaces are optimized for tasks like modeling, animation, and video editing. Workspaces are only an interface arrangement and won't affect 3D data.

How to save an existing interface as a new Workspace? You can easily keep an existing layout as a new Workspace by clicking the "+" icon at the top of your 3D Viewport and choosing "Duplicate Current." Choosing this option creates a new tab at the top of your interface. You can double-click the tab to assign a unique name to that Workspace.

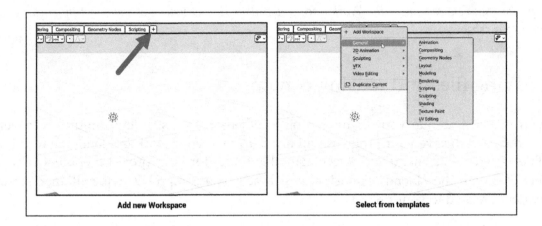

Add new Workspace   **Select from templates**

Figure 1.8 - *Workspace selector*

The tabs you see at the top represent just a fraction of the many Workspaces that Blender has to offer. By clicking on the plus icon, you can explore and select from a variety of predefined Workspaces, categorized under headings such as General, 2D Animation, and so forth. Upon selecting one, a new tab will emerge in the user interface, unveiling your chosen Workspace.

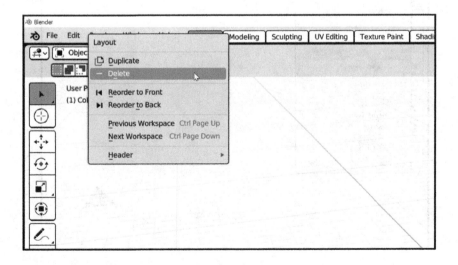

Figure 1.9 - *Managing Workspaces*

To remove a Workspace from your user interface, you can *right-click* on the Workspace name and choose the "Delete" option (Figure 1.9).

Tip: *You can also rearrange the Workspace order at the top of your 3D Viewport by clicking and dragging the tabs.*

1.2 Saving files and reusing content

As you invest time into your Blender project, whether it's just a few minutes or several hours, the need to save your progress will arise. To save your work in Blender, navigate to the File → Save As… menu and select a suitable folder for your project file. Blender saves project files with the ".blend" extension, which acts as a comprehensive container, storing every detail related to your project.

Sometimes, you will also see additional files in your folder with extensions like ".blend1", which are backup copies from your projects that Blender automatically creates.

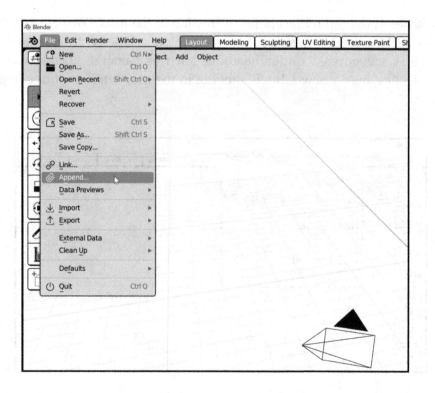

Figure 1.10 - Append and Link

In addition to protecting your data, saving a project in Blender significantly benefits reusability. From 3D models to Workspaces, a wide range of data stored in a Blender file can be seamlessly incorporated into subsequent projects, augmenting efficiency and continuity.

For instance, if you made a useful Workspace that you want to reuse in a new project. You can quickly get that Workspace using the *Append* or *Link* options from the File menu (Figure 1.10).

The Append option incorporates data into a new file, which merges the information into your current project. The Link option creates a relative connection to the original project file saved. It means the data won't stay at your current project but in the external Blender file where you pulled the asset.

If you want to make changes the asset, like a material or 3D model, you should pick the Append option. For the cases where you don't need to edit the data, use the Link option.

For instance, to get a Workspace from another Blender file saved in your hard drive, go to the **File → Append** menu and locate the file. Once you click on the filename, you will see a list of folders (Figure 1.11).

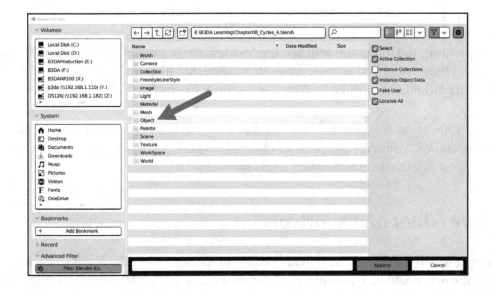

Figure 1.11 - *Folders for Append*

Each folder has a type of data you can pull from the file. One folder has the name Work-Space; inside, you will see a list of all your existing Workspaces for that file. Select the Workspace you want and press the "Append" button (Figure 1.12).

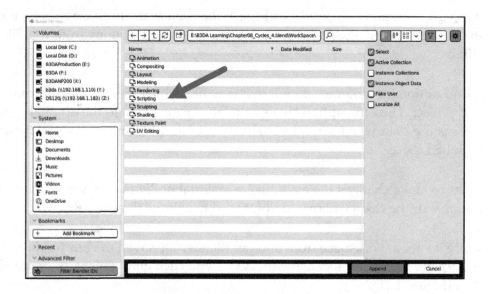

Figure 1.12 - *Workspaces in folder*

After appending the data, you will see the Workspace in your user interface. The process applies to all other assets you want to bring from external files. You can use the Append option to pull 3D models, materials, textures, animation, or anything else you wish to reuse.

Info: As you might see from the Append tool example, assigning meaningful names inside Blender is imperative. Whenever you have an object that you want to use later in future projects, it will make it much easier to locate important assets by name.

1.3 Active editor and shortcuts

Before diving into the shortcuts and 3D Navigation tools within Blender, it's crucial to grasp the idea of the *active Editor*. This concept determines where Blender applies a specific tool or option when activated via a shortcut.

What exactly is the active Editor? Simply put, it's the Editor where your mouse cursor resides when you invoke a shortcut. For example, if your mouse cursor hovers over the 3D

Viewport and you press a key, Blender will interpret and execute that command within the context of the 3D Viewport.

1.3.1 Active editors example

Understanding the significance of the *active Editor* is essential, especially when using short-cuts that target a specific function within a designated Editor. Take, for instance, the task of deleting a keyframe within an Editor named *Timeline*. To remove data from the Timeline, you must position your mouse cursor over the Timeline Editor. If you use the shortcut without the Timeline being the active Editor, Blender won't delete the keyframe.

In Blender, pressing the *X key* or *DELETE* serves the purpose of removal. Both these shortcuts can be used to eliminate various data types, be it 3D models or keyframes. Now, imagine a scenario where you have both a 3D model highlighted and a keyframe present in the Timeline. If you press the DELETE key, which of the two will Blender remove?

The answer lies in the position of your mouse cursor. If it's hovering over the 3D Viewport, the 3D model will disappear from your workspace. On the other hand, if you want to delete the keyframe, ensure you press the key while the cursor is positioned over the Timeline.

The concept of an active Editor is essential for all shortcuts in Blender. You can choose where to apply a keyboard shortcut with the active Editor.

1.4 3D Navigation and Zoom controls

The 3D Viewport is the most important Editor in the Blender user interface regarding modeling and visualization of 3D data. In this Editor, we can use several tools and shortcuts to navigate the 3D space. Blender uses a combination of mouse and keyboard shortcuts to navigate in 3D.

Here is a list of the most common shortcuts for 3D Navigation:

- **Middle mouse button**: Press and hold the button and move the Cursor to start rotating your view.
- **SHIFT+ Middle mouse button**: Press the keys and drag your mouse to move your screen (Pan).

– **CTRL+Middle mouse button**: Press both keys and move your mouse up and down to zoom in and out.

– **Numpad 5**: Swap between orthographic and perspective projections.

– **Numpad 1**: Front view

– **Numpad 3**: Right view

– **Numpad 7**: Top view

– **Home key**: Zoom all objects in your scene

Regarding orthographic views, we have to use an additional key to change the view to Back, Left, or Bottom. Press the CTRL key alongside each Numpad 1, 3, and 7 to get the corresponding opposite view. For instance, you will get the Left View by pressing the CTRL+Numpad 3.

An easy and fast way to navigate in 3D involves the backquote key from your keyboard. After pressing the ` key, a pie menu appears will multiple options to change your current view (Figure 1.13).

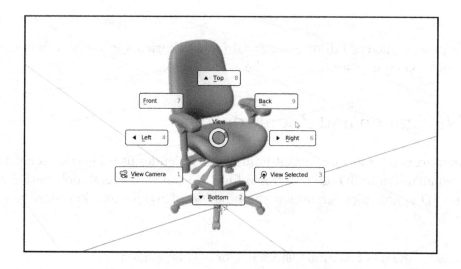

Figure 1.13 - *Pie Menu with view options*

That pie menu shows options with all orthographic views and a couple more. For instance, it is possible to jump straight into the active camera view or "View Selected." This last option lets your 3D Viewport zoom in and focus on any selected objects.

With the backquote shortcut, you can quickly navigate without needing a numeric keyboard entry. However, a numeric keyboard (*Numpad*) is still essential to navigate in 3D. For instance, using the **Numpad 5** is the quickest way to swap between a perspective and orthographic projections.

What if you don't have a keyboard with a Numpad? You can emulate the Numpad functions using the **Edit → Preferences...** menu and going to the Input tab (Figure 1.14).

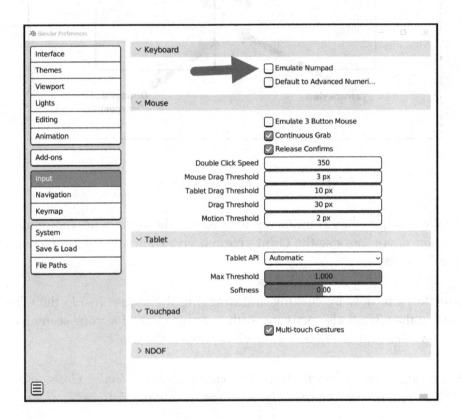

Figure 1.14 - *Emulate Numpad*

There you will find an option to emulate the Numpad. After enabling the "Emulate Numpad." The alphanumeric keys will work like the numeric keyboard. Notice that you also have an option to control *Multi-touch Gestures* at the bottom of the panel.

1.4.1 3D Navigation buttons

Besides those shortcuts, you also have navigation buttons on the top right of your 3D Viewport. They will help you with a mouse, only 3D Navigation (Figure 1.15).

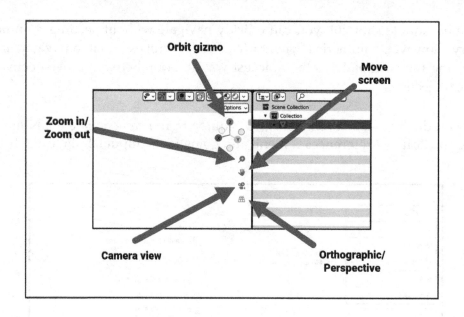

Figure 1.15 - *Navigation buttons*

The navigation buttons have similar options to the shortcuts with the mouse and keyboard. For instance, you can use the Orbit gizmo if you want a more interactive way to go around in the 3D space.

You can rotate your view by clicking and dragging the mouse inside the Gizmo. Using the circles inside the Gizmo also activates orthographic views for your scene. For instance, using the circle with a Z inside makes your view jump to the top.

Info: *All navigation and zoom controls work on most Editors in Blender. Unless they don't share the same data type, for instance, you can only use 3D rotation in the Viewport.*

1.5 Object selection

If you've opted for the *left mouse button* as your primary selection tool during the Quick Setup, that's the button you'll employ throughout Blender for all selection-related tasks. This consistency applies across the 3D Viewport and other Editors, ensuring uniformity in selection methods and shortcuts.

Here are some straightforward ways to select objects in Blender:

– A mere single click will do the job, irrespective of the Editor you're in.

- To select multiple objects simultaneously, press and hold the SHIFT key.

- While holding the SHIFT key, left-click on various objects to either add them to or exclude them from your current selection.

What visual cue indicates a selected object in the 3D Viewport? The answer is a vibrant orange outline that graces every selected item, signaling Blender's way of showcasing your active selection (Figure 1.16).

Figure 1.16 - *Outline showing a select object*

When multiple objects are highlighted, you'll observe that the most recently selected object display a more vivid outline. This is a unique feature in Blender known as the active object. Essentially, the active object is the last item you've added to your selection.

Info: From this point forward, I will assume you choose the left button for selection. Whenever I mention a selection, you will perform it using a left click.

Managing your active object when selecting multiple items is crucial. This is especially true for tasks that require interaction with multiple objects simultaneously. Take, for example, the process of creating parenting relationships between objects in animation projects. In such scenarios, the active object invariably assumes the role of the primary or dominant object.

It is possible to turn any object from a selection into the active one. After selecting multiple objects, hold the SHIFT key, and click on any of the selected objects. This object assume the role of active, in the context of that selection.

How to remove an object from a selection? Hold the SHIFT key and double-click at any object. The first click makes the object active, and the second removes it from the selection. One click will be enough if you are trying to remove the active object from the selection.

Here is a summary of your selection shortcuts:

– **SHIFT+Left-Click**: Add objects to the selection

– **SHIFT+Left-Click (with selected objects)**: Turn the object active in the selection

– **SHIFT+Left-Click (In the active object)**: Remove it from the selection

– **SHIFT+Left-Click twice (Any object but the active)**: Remove an object from the selection

As you can see from the list, you will handle most of the selections using a combination of a *Left-Click* and the *SHIFT key*. There are also some crucial shortcuts for object selection:

– **B key**: Makes a box selection, which draws a rectangular shape in your interface. To select a group of objects, you can draw a box around them. Holding the SHIFT key while drawing the box removes the objects from the selection.

– **A key**: Add all objects to the selection if you don't have anything selected.

– **ALT+A**: Removes all objects from a selection.

– **CTRL+I**: Invert the selection, which is a great way to get multiple objects selected and leave just a few unselected.

Besides selection shortcuts, you will find a few options to select objects in the 3D Viewport Toolbar (Figure 1.17). If you click and hold the "Select Box" icon, you expand the button to display all options related to selection.

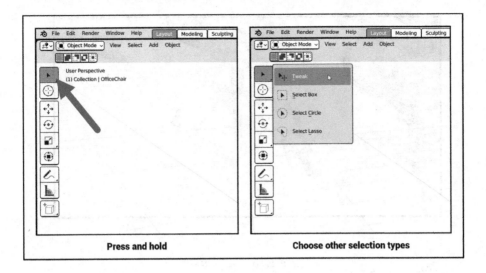

| Press and hold | Choose other selection types |

Figure 1.17 - Toolbar options

With the select circle, you can "paint" a selection by clicking and dragging the small circle that will appear on your screen. The lasso lets you draw a shape that adds all objects inside to the selection.

Info: A significant aspect of the selection shortcuts is that you can use them in all editors. The same keys work regardless of the Editor you have at the moment.

1.6 The 3D Cursor

A core element of the Blender user interface is the 3D Cursor, a small crosshair icon you find in the 3D Viewport. The Cursor has an essential role in using Blender (Figure 1.18).

With the 3D Cursor, you can:

– Set the location where you create 3D objects

– Move objects to a specific location

– Work as a temporary pivot point for rotation and scaling

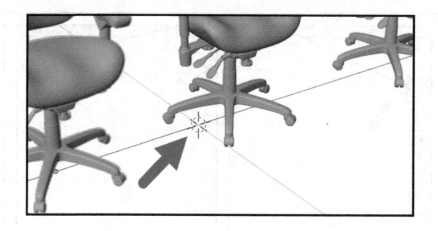

Figure 1.18 - 3D Cursor

Those are a few use cases for the 3D Cursor, which you employ extensively for modeling and object manipulation. Since that is a core function of Blender, you must learn how to move and align the Cursor around the 3D Viewport.

1.6.1 Moving the 3D Cursor

The 3D Cursor is vital for several tasks related to modeling and manipulating objects, and you must know how to move it around. You can easily set the location of your 3D Cursor using the mouse.

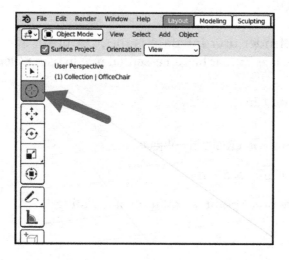

Figure 1.19 - 3D Cursor in the Toolbar

Hold the SHIFT key and right-click anywhere in your 3D Viewport to set a new 3D Cursor location. There is even an option at the 3D Viewport Toolbar that will enable you to left-click without the SHIFT key to set a new location for the 3D Cursor (Figure 1.19).

Even with those options to quickly move your 3D Cursor using the mouse, you may want more control over the cursor location.

You can precisely control the 3D Cursor location using the Sidebar of your 3D Viewport. By pressing the *N key*, you will open the Sidebar, and at the View tab, you will find the 3D Cursor options (Figure 1.20).

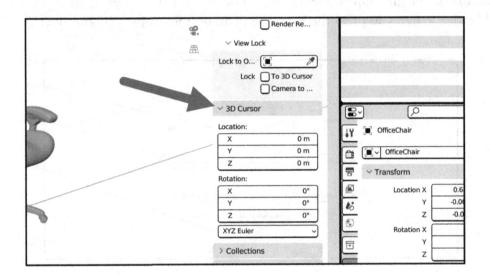

Figure 1.20 - *3D Cursor options*

There you can change the values for both location and rotation of your 3D Cursor. An important shortcut to handle the 3D Cursor is the *SHIFT+C*, which will center the 3D Cursor in your 3D Viewport and align your view to the Cursor.

The shortcut works like a reset for the 3D Cursor, and you should use it whenever you want to get it back to the origin point of your 3D Viewport.

Tip: The 3D Viewport features a Sidebar to its right, which can be toggled open or closed with the N key. Similarly, the Toolbar on the left has its own shortcut: the T key. This functionality of having both a Sidebar and a Toolbar is consistent across most Editors in Blender.

1.6.2 Using the Snap for the 3D Cursor

Using the selection tools and our 3D Cursor, we can move objects in the 3D Viewport with the Snap options of Blender. What is the Snap? It is a collection of tools that feature options to align and move particular objects using a combination of the 3D Cursor and object origins.

For instance, you can get a selected object to move to the exact location as your 3D Cursor. You can also align the Cursor with an object location.

You can use either the **Object** → **Snap** menu or the SHIFT+S keys to view your Snap options in Blender. When you press the keys, the Snap options appear (Figure 1.21).

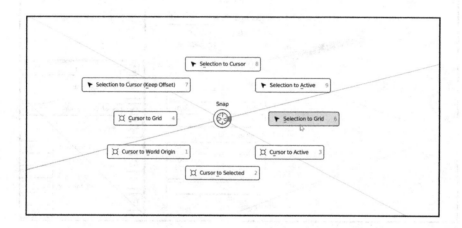

Figure 1.21 - Snap options

At the Snap, you will find the following options:

- **Selection to Cursor**: Move the selected object to the 3D Cursor location.

- **Selection to Active**: Move the selected object to the same position as your active object.

- **Selection to Grid**: Align the selected object to the grid lines at the base of your 3D Viewport.

- **Cursor to Active**: Align the 3D Cursor to the Active object.

- **Cursor to Selected**: Move the 3D Cursor to the same location as your selected object.

- **Cursor to World Origin**: Move the 3D Cursor to the zero coordinate for X, Y, and Z.

- **Cursor to Grid**: Align the 3D Cursor to the grid lines at the base of your 3D Viewport.

- **Selection to Cursor (Keep offset)**: Moves the selected object to the 3D Cursor location and keeps the positions relative to each vertex of your 3D model. We will cover more about vertex manipulation in Chapter 3.

How to use the Snap to manipulate objects? You can move any selected objects to the 3D Cursor location using the Snap. For instance, we can take the scene shown in Figure 1.22.

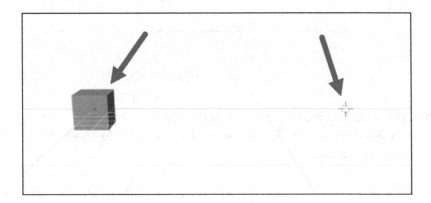

Figure 1.22 - Using the Snap

We have an object at the scene far from the 3D Cursor. If you press the SHIFT+S keys and from the Snap options choose **Selection to Cursor**, you will make the object "jump" to the location of your 3D Cursor (Figure 1.23).

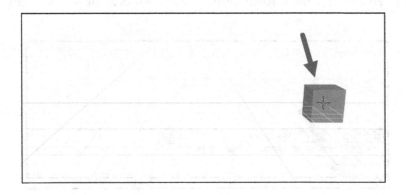

Figure 1.23 - Object aligned to 3D Cursor

You can also choose the **Cursor to Selection** to make your 3D Cursor move to the object location (Figure 1.24).

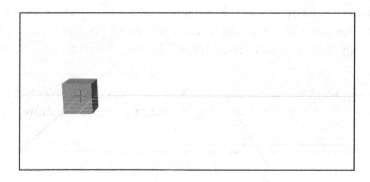

Figure 1.24 - *3D Cursor aligned to the object*

Having a tool dedicated to moving objects in the 3D Viewport may look simple now. But you will see the importance of the 3D Cursor when we start to work with object creation and modeling in chapters 2 and 3.

Info: Origin Point is the reference point for object locations in Blender. We will learn how to manipulate and control those points in Chapter 2.

1.7 Using the status bar

We have a helpful status bar at the bottom of your user interface to give you additional information about a tool or the current scene. For instance, pressing the B key to start a box selection provide you with some information or other options for that tool (Figure 1.25).

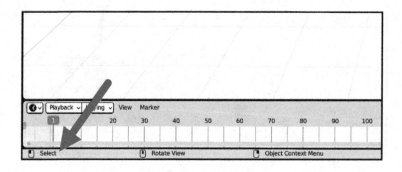

Figure 1.25 - *Additional tools and options*

Those additional tools and options appear on the left side of the status bar, and it adapts to the tool you are currently using. Always keep an eye there to find new shortcuts and options.

On the right side, we have, by default, only the Blender version. You can add more information by right-clicking there to open a small menu (Figure 1.26).

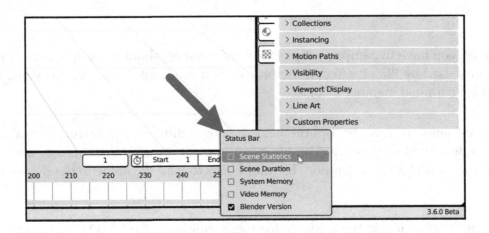

Figure 1.26 - *Status bar information*

For instance, if you enable all options from the menu, you will have some helpful information about the Blender file displayed (Figure 1.27).

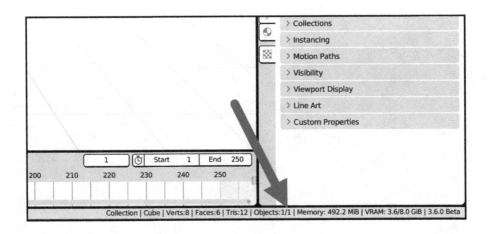

Figure 1.27 - *Scene information*

There you have a list with statistics about your 3D models like:

– Objects

– Faces

– Triangles

– Vertices

Besides that, you have two important pieces of information about the scene. One is the current memory used by Blender to edit the project. You can keep an eye on this value in systems that have limited memory available.

The VRAM amount is another option that can make a difference later during rendering. If you have a dedicated graphics card on your computer, it has a total amount of memory. To render a scene with GPU acceleration, Blender needs to load the scene to the device memory.

The scene must fit inside the memory for processing, and the VRAM information helps you keep track of that limit. If it doesn't fit, you must render the scene with CPU only, which is usually slower.

You only see the VRAM value in Blender if you have a dedicated graphics card and a driver that gives access to that information.

What is next?

Having journeyed through this chapter, you've laid the foundation by understanding Blender's user interface and the crux of its features. The versatility of the Editors not only shapes tasks but also tailors the interface, making Blender uniquely adaptable. Your initiation into the realm of 3D space navigation and Blender file data management is a testimony to your progress.

Drawing an aviation analogy, envision this chapter as your pre-flight checklist, acquainting you with the cockpit controls of your aircraft. You're now primed for takeoff. And just as a pilot may occasionally refer to the manual, don't hesitate to revisit this chapter, especially as you familiarize yourself with the plethora of shortcuts.

As we pave the way for Chapter 2, here's a glimpse of what awaits you. Building upon the foundational concepts acquired, we'll dive deeper into object creation and metamorphosis. Until now, our sandbox has been limited to Blender's default elements. But the horizon expands in the upcoming chapter, as we delve into crafting new objects, and subsequently, morphing them using Blender's coveted Edit Mode.

Concluding our first chapter, it's imperative to emphasize that mastering software is akin to an expedition. With Blender, as with any voyage, there will be moments of bewilderment and challenges. Yet, my commitment remains steadfast—to equip you with increasing proficiency and confidence, sculpting a gradual and enriching learning curve, with the endgame being your seamless mastery of Blender by this guide's conclusion.

Chapter 2 - Object Creation and Manipulation

At the core of 3D design lies a pivotal process: modeling. With your newfound familiarity of the Blender user interface, Chapter 2 beckons you to breathe life into your concepts through 3D object creation—a central theme of this section.

Fashioning objects in Blender isn't merely about clicking and selecting; it's a series of decisions that steer simple shapes towards intricate designs. We commence by delving into the different object categories available in Blender and understanding the pivotal role of the 3D Cursor in the genesis of these objects. Upon introducing new objects to the 3D Viewport, we'll morph them using fundamental operations.

Grasp the art of moving, rotating, and resizing objects—elementary yet potent maneuvers in 3D design. And, understanding that to err is human, we'll demystify the Undo History, guiding you to seamlessly backtrack when a design decision doesn't pan out.

Concluding this chapter, we'll familiarize you with work modes, spotlighting the Edit Mode. For those envisaging extensive 3D modeling ventures in Blender, Edit Mode is paramount—it's the heartland of modeling projects. You'll also acquire skills to orchestrate scenes using Collections and navigate using the Asset Browser.

Here's a summary of what you will learn:

- How to create objects in Blender.

- Mastering object transformations, including duplicating objects and numeric transformations.

- The art of undoing and redoing actions in Blender.

- Understanding and navigating through different work modes.

- The concept and importance of object origins, including pivot points and transformations.

- The essential process of creating and managing object collections.

- Using the Asset Browser to create and utilize your asset library.

2.1 Creating objects in Blender

To create objects in Blender, use the **Add** menu at the 3D Viewport header or the SHIFT+A keys. The shortcut works for object creation with the 3D Viewport as the active Editor. If you need to remember how Active Editors works, refer to Chapter 1 and reread Section 1.3.

By pressing SHIFT+A or opening the Add menu, you will see a box with all creation options for Blender (Figure 2.1).

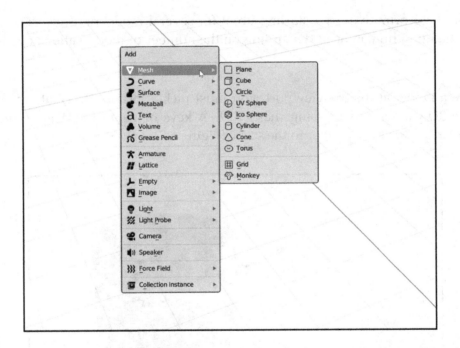

Figure 2.1 - *Object creation box*

You find options to add different objects in that menu, starting with polygons under the Mesh group and others like cameras, lights, and even Collection instances. Depending on the project in Blender, you might need a particular type of object. To start with 3D modeling, the most straightforward type to create and manage is a Mesh object (Polygon).

At the Mesh group, you can create geometrical primitives such as:

– Plane

- Cube

- Circle

- UV Sphere (square faces)

- ICO Sphere (triangular facer)

- Cylinder

- Cone

- Torus

We can use those primitives as a starting point for several modeling projects. A Cube can become a chair or a human head depending on the number of modifications applied to the object.

To create a model at the 3D Viewport, you must pick a location to create the object by placing the 3D Cursor and pressing the SHIFT+A keys or using the Add menu. For instance, we can add a new Cylinder to the scene (Figure 2.2).

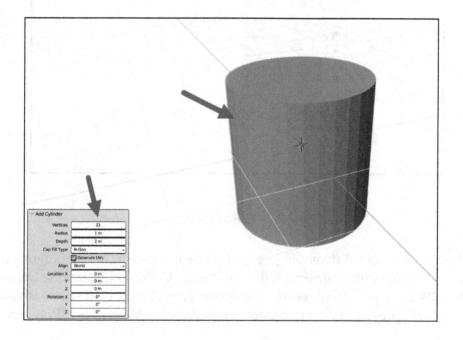

Figure 2.2 - *Cylinder at the scene*

A critical aspect of object creation is that whenever you add an object to the 3D Viewport, a small menu appears at the lower-left corner of your 3D Viewport. That menu displays some contextual information regarding the created object.

For instance, when you create a Cylinder, it is possible to edit aspects of the object like:

- **Vertices**: The number of sides for the cylinder.

- **Radius**: Distance from the center to the border.

- **Depth**: The height of your cylinder.

If you plan or need to change the object based on that contextual menu, you must do it right after the object creation. If you select anything else or perform another operation, that menu disappears.

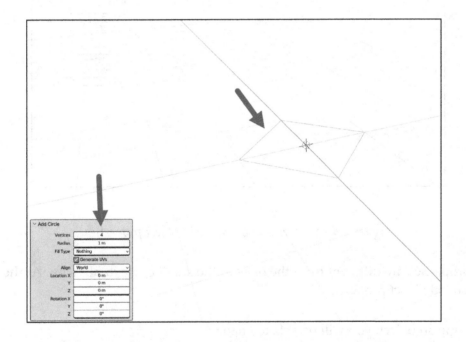

Figure 2.3 - Square from circle

In some cases, you must use the menu to make adjustments to the object. For instance, you can create a square from a Circle. Create a Circle from the Mesh group and set your Vertices option to four (Figure 2.3).

That results in a square, similar to a Mesh Plane with only border edges.

Tip: If you accidentally close the menu by selecting other objects, you can call it back by pressing the F9 key. However, it will only work if you don't perform any other operation. The F9 key calls the "Adjust last operation..." option. Blender is not parametric, and for that reason, you can only make changes to object properties during the creation process.

For each object created in Blender, you can view and edit some of their properties straight in the 3D Viewport. For that, use the Sidebar by pressing the N key (Figure 2.4).

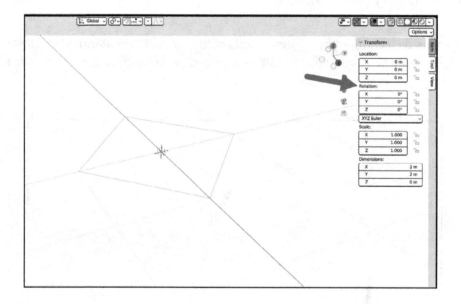

Figure 2.4 - Sidebar to view and edit object properties

Those properties are different from the ones in the small contextual menu. At the Sidebar, you get general object properties.

By selecting an object, you will be able to change:

– Location

– Rotation

– Scale

Each property has numeric values that can receive updates in each respective field. For instance, you can rotate an object in the Z-axis 45 degrees by entering that value in the Rotation field identified with the Z letter.

Tip: When you press the N key to expand the 3D Viewport Sidebar, your mouse cursor must be above the 3D Viewport Editor. Other Editors also feature Sidebars with different properties.

You will also find the same options in the Properties Editor, where you have the Object Properties tab (Figure 2.5).

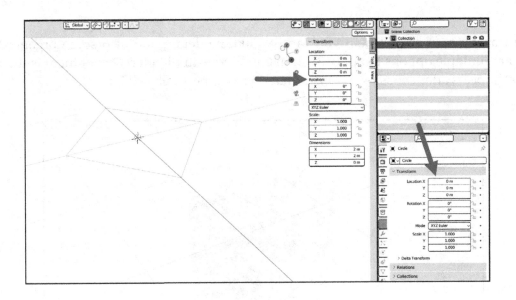

Figure 2.5 - Properties Editor

Both options display information based on the selected objects. The Sidebar has a shorter list of options, whereas with the Properties Editor, you will get extended options to edit objects spread across multiple tabs.

Tip: Regardless of the method, you can activate an interesting tool to protect objects from receiving transformations. You can enable the small padlock icon for each transformation to protect them from any unintentional changes.

2.2 Object transformations

After creating objects in Blender, you can transform them in the 3D Viewport. In any software that supports the handling of 3D Data, you will most likely find three main types of transformations:

- Move

- Rotate

- Scale

Those transformations will help you in tasks like modeling and also scene organization. There are multiple options to apply 3D transformations in Blender. One of them is the widget that appears after choosing a transformation from the Toolbar (Figure 2.6).

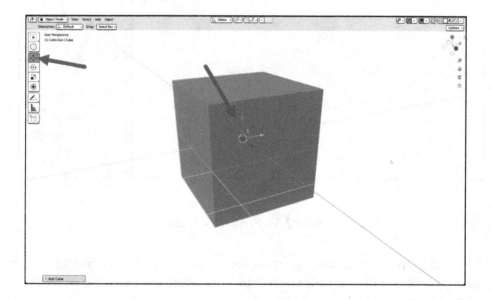

Figure 2.6 - Transform gizmo

The gizmo icon changes based on the transformation type you choose from the Toolbar. Each gizmo allows interaction with a selected object in a certain way:

- **Move**: Click and drag the mouse on the arrow corresponding to the axis in which you want to move the object.

- **Rotate**: Click and drag the mouse in the arc representing the axis you want to use for a rotation.

- **Scale**: Click and drag in the small squares at the end of each line representing an axis.

A quick way to change the gizmo type is with the SHIFT+SPACEBAR keys. Pressing those keys in the 3D Viewport will open a small menu with shortcuts for all three transformations. There is also an option named Transform, which will create a "super" widget with all three operations appearing simultaneously.

Tip: You can toggle the 3D Viewport Toolbar using the T key. By default, you will only see vertical icons in the Toolbar, but you can expand it by placing the mouse cursor at the right border of your icons. You can click and drag to expand once it turns to a double-sided arrow.

Even with the widget offering a visual tool to apply transformations, you will find that most Blender artists prefer to use keyboard shortcuts to perform transformations. You can quickly implement a transformation using the following shortcuts:

- **G key**: Move an object

- **R key**: Rotate an object

- **S key**: Scale an object

Once you trigger a transformation using those keys, move your mouse cursor to update the selection properties, and click somewhere in the 3D Viewport to finish an operation. For instance, select one or multiple objects and press the G key. By moving your mouse cursor, all selected objects follows the same movement. With a left click, you confirm the new location for your group of objects.

You can cancel the transformation at any moment by pressing the ESC key.

Tip: Those keys work in all editors for transformations. For instance, you can move animation data in the Timeline using the G key.

As you experiment further, you'll notice that when using a hotkey to initiate a transformation, it gets applied across all axes simultaneously. This contrasts with the widget method, where objects in the 3D Viewport move with axis constraints, and you can select an axis by its color to limit the transformation.

However, there's a method to restrict transformations to a specific axis using hotkeys. Simply press the key corresponding to your desired axis after initiating the transformation. For example, to move an object along the X-axis, press the X key right after pressing the G key.

Here are some examples of keys that apply transformations with an axis constraint:

- **G key followed by the Y key**: Move in the Y-axis

- **R key followed by the Z key**: Rotate in the Z-axis

- **S key followed by the X key**: Scale in the X-axis

Notice that you should press the keys in sequence and not simultaneously. You can use any combination of those keys to apply a transformation.

Tip: *Pressing the ESC key can always cancel the current transformation.*

The **Object → Transformations** menu also offers all transformation options. You will find a list of additional tools for object transformation in Blender.

2.2.1 Duplicating objects

In Blender, you will find that some operations automatically trigger a transformation. For instance, duplicating an object in your 3D Viewport will also move the copied object to a new location. You can use the same shortcuts and options from transformations, like constraining them to a single axis.

First, how to duplicate an object? You can copy any object with the SHIFT+D keys with an object selected or the **Object → Duplicate Objects** menu. For instance, you can choose one or multiple objects and press the SHIFT+D keys. By moving the mouse cursor, you will start to see the duplicates. Click anywhere in your 3D Viewport to place your newly created objects.

If you want to create a more ordinated set of copies, you can press a key corresponding to an axis in your keyboard right after pressing SHIFT+D. You can make multiple copies of objects on the X-axis using the X key right after pressing SHIFT+D (Figure 2.7).

Figure 2.7 - *Copies in the X-axis*

Using the SHIFT+D keys gives you a lot of freedom to create all kinds of copies based on the type of selection you have in Blender. For instance, you can start making multiple copies from a selection of various objects simultaneously.

There is also another option for duplicating objects called Linked Duplicate. You make an instance of your selected object by making a linked copy. Any changes applied to one object propagate to all copies. Use the ALT+D to create a linked copy.

To unlink any duplicates created with the ALT+D, use the **Object → Relations → Make Single User → Object & Data** menu. Select the copied object and use that menu option.

Info: For some operations, you should create a copy of an object in the same location as your original selection. By pressing the ESC key after SHIFT+D, you create the duplicate but cancel the move transformation. That results in your objects staying at the same locations.

2.2.2 Numeric transformations

One option that you can use in Blender to enhance your transformations is to use numeric values to set distances, rotations, and scale factors. Whenever you trigger a transformation in Blender, you can type in your keyboard to assign precise values for that particular transformation.

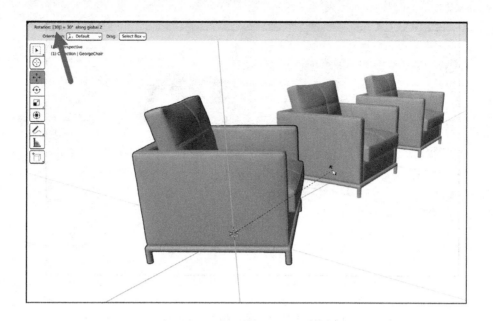

Figure 2.8 - Rotation values

For instance, you can press the R key to rotate and limit it to the Z-axis (Z key), and once you move the mouse, values for that rotation will appear at the status bar of the 3D Viewport (Figure 2.8).

Figure 2.9 - Rotation with fixed value

Notice that this is a different status bar on the top left of your 3D Viewport. Back in Chapter 1, we saw the status bar dedicated to displaying information about the project and tools at the bottom of your interface.

If you type a value like 45 and press RETURN before clicking anywhere, you set the rotation to a precise value of 45 degrees. With numeric transformations, you can also use expressions. Before typing the expression, press the = Key, and use an expression like "15*3" to get a transformation with 45 (Figure 2.9).

You can verify the rotation amount in the Sidebar. Look to the Rotation field with the object selected, and it should display 45 on your Z-axis. You can also change that transformation by setting a different value in the Sidebar.

The same applies to a move transformation, where you can:

1. Select an object

2. Press the G key to move

3. Press the X key to constrain it to the X-axis

4. Type 5

5. Press RETURN to finish the transformation

With this sequence, your object move five units on the X-axis. You can also use negative values by typing -5 to go in the opposite direction.

With the scale, you must use a factor to control object sizes. For instance, a factor of 1 means 100% of the object size. If you want to increase the size by 50%, use a factor of 1.5 for the scale. To reduce the size by 30%, use 0.7 as a factor.

The sequence to increase the size by 50% would be:

1. Select an object

2. Press the S key to start a scaling transformation

3. Type 1.5

4. Press RETURN to finish the transformation

Notice how we did not constrain the scale to any axis in the sequence, but you could also press a key corresponding to an axis after the S key.

Tip: *You can use either the Sidebar of your 3D Viewport or the Object Properties tab at the Properties Editor to change those values. But editing with keyboard shortcuts will be much faster.*

2.3 Undoing and Redoing in Blender

How to undo a transformation in Blender? Like most softwares, we also have an Undo option in Blender, which you can use with the CTRL+Z keys. There is an option to trigger the Undo with the **Edit → Undo** menu.

To go back and redo an action, you can use the Redo option, which works using the SHIFT+CTRL+Z keys. Another valuable tool in Blender is the Repeat Last option, which you can trigger using the SHIFT+R keys.

The Repeat Last can become helpful in some modeling tasks. For instance, if you move an object six units in the X-axis and press SHIFT+R, you will get the same operation repeated.

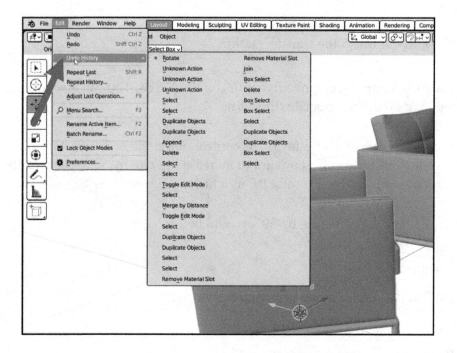

Figure 2.10 - *Undo history*

Instead of applying a single move transformation, you can press SHIFT+R multiple times to repeat the operation.

An essential option for undoing and redoing involves the editing history Blender keeps for each file you work at. Open the editing history using the **Edit → Undo History**. By choosing that option, you see a list of all recent actions from that file (Figure 2.10).

Suppose you click on any of those actions, and Blender jumps back to that state of your project. That is an easy and fast way to undo multiple steps at once.

In addition to that option, you can also control the number of steps Blender keeps in the Undo History. Open the **Edit → Preferences** menu and go to the System tab (Figure 2.11).

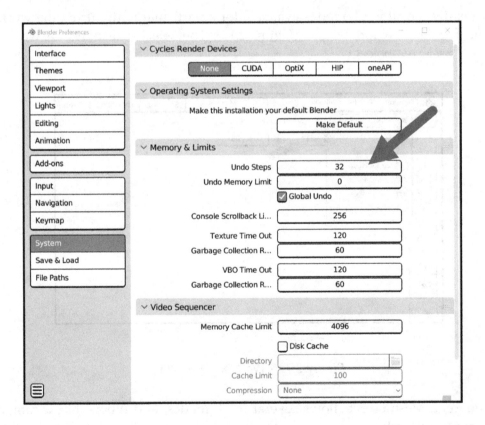

Figure 2.11 - *System options*

There you will find an option called Undo Steps, which starts with 32 as the default value. Increasing that number will make Blender keep more actions and use more memory from your computer. Unless you have a good reason to increase that value, it is wise to leave it with the default number.

Tip: Even with the option to work with an undo history. It would help to keep a healthy habit of saving your project as much as possible. That prevents you from losing data.

2.4 Work modes

Most entities in Blender, like 3D objects, feature different work modes. Until now, you probably used only Object Mode for general object manipulation. Besides Object Mode, we have other modes like Edit Mode, Sculpt Mode, and Texture Paint.

You can easily see all work modes available for a particular entity using the work mode selector in the 3D Viewport header (Figure 2.12). The selector displays all work modes available for a selected object.

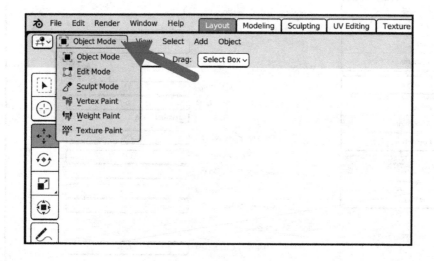

Figure 2.12 - Work mode selector

For instance, a Mesh object shows several work modes, and others, like a camera, will only feature Object Mode.

With work modes, we can access unique tools and options for object manipulation. For Mesh objects, you have Edit Mode, where we can perform a significant amount of 3D Modeling in Blender.

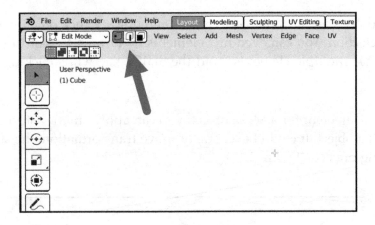

Figure 2.13 - *Mesh element selector*

Once you select any Mesh object and change the work mode to Edit, you start to see the structure of that selected object. The Toolbar on the left displays options related to that Mode, and you will be able to view and manipulate:

– Vertices

– Edges

– Faces

You can easily change the type of element you wish to edit for that polygon using the buttons on the right of your work mode selector (Figure 2.13).

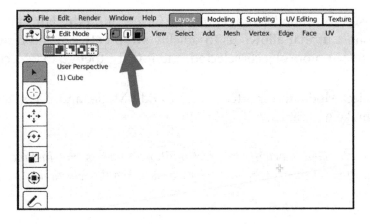

Figure 2.14 - *Mixing elements*

For instance, you can set the tool to select faces and quickly click on any face of a polygon to add it to the selection. You can even mix elements by turning two or three modes simultaneously. To enable multiple elements, hold the SHIFT key while clicking on each button (Figure 2.14).

After selecting an element for a Mesh object, you can apply any transformation to change the structure of that object. It could be a scale or move transformation, the starting point for many 3D modeling projects (Figure 2.15).

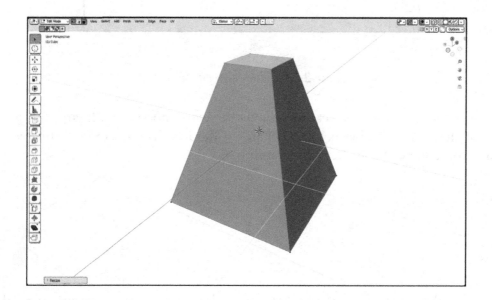

Figure 2.15 - *Object transformation*

The two most used work modes in Blender are Object and Edit. For that reason, you will find a dedicated shortcut that allows us to quickly swap between those two modes. Press the TAB key with one or more objects selected, and it will either go to Object or Edit Modes.

If you are in Object Mode, the shortcut swap to Edit Mode, and if you are in Edit Mode, the TAB key will make you return to Object Mode.

Info: *You can use the same shortcuts to select multiple elements. For instance, you can hold the SHIFT key to add multiple elements (vertices, edges, or faces) to the selection.*

2.5 Object origins

Before working with 3D modeling in Blender, it is vital to understand and learn how to manipulate some critical properties of objects in the 3D Viewport. One of those aspects is the object origin point, which might help you place and edit 3D models with improved precision.

Where are object origins? You will find that most 3D objects in Blender display a small dot with an solid color (Figure 2.16).

Figure 2.16 - Object origin

Every time you set the coordinates of an object using either the Sidebar or the Properties Editor, you use the origin point location as the reference. If you select the coordinates as zero for all axis, the origin point will stay at those coordinates.

For instance, when you create a Cube object with the 3D Cursor at the origin of your scene, which has a zero value for all 3D axis, you will have the Cube placed at the exact center of your scene (Figure 2.17).

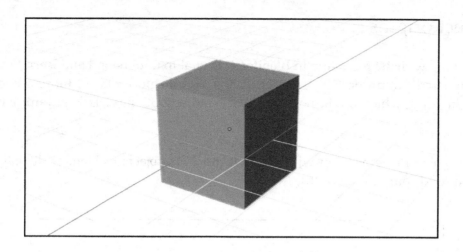

Figure 2.17 - Cube at exact center

Since the origin point for the Cube is in the middle of the object, you have an object with the bottom half below the "ground plane" if you consider that your Z-axis zero level is the ground or floor for your scene (Figure 2.18).

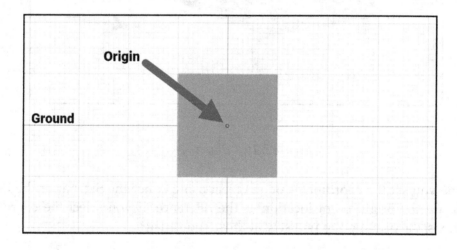

Figure 2.18 - Object at ground level

That won't help in tasks where you must align and place an object on the "ground floor" for modeling. We can easily change and edit the origin point location using a combination of our 3D Cursor and the Snap options.

The Snap options provide a suite of shortcuts that allow you to align and position the 3D Cursor based on a selected object. Interestingly, the 3D Cursor can be employed as a reference to determine a fresh location for the model's origin point. This grants us a useful tool for positioning the origin point at crucial spots.

For instance, we can place the origin point at the base of the Cube using a simple procedure:

1. Select the Cube and go to Edit Mode

2. Change the selection mode to face

3. Select the bottom Face of your Cube

4. Press SHIFT+S and choose *Cursor to Selected*

With that procedure, you will get the 3D Cursor aligned to the bottom face of your Cube (Figure 2.19).

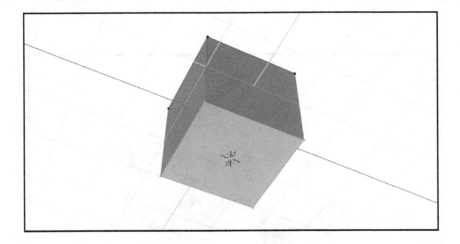

Figure 2.19 - *3D Cursor aligned to the Cube*

After you align the 3D Cursor, return to Object Mode and use the **Object → Set Origin** menu. There you have an option called **Origin to 3D Cursor**. If you choose that option, you can change the location of your origin point to the same location as your 3D Cursor (Figure 2.20).

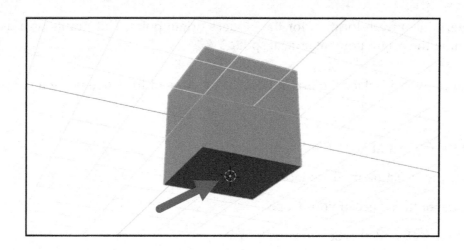

Figure 2.20 - *Origin point location*

If you try to set a Z coordinate value of the Cube to zero, it will become aligned to the "ground level" of your scene.

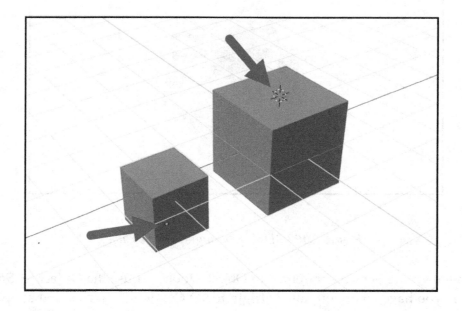

Figure 2.21 - *Cubes for alignment*

You can also use this same technique to place objects in the scene. For instance, we easily place a Cube with an origin point at its bottom face on top of another Cube or any other object. Ensure the 3D Cursor is at the exact location where you want to align the object to use this procedure.

In that case, we have the Cube with the origin point at the bottom and another larger Cube with the 3D Cursor aligned to the top face (Figure 2.21).

Select the Cube you wish to move, press SHIFT+S, and pick *Selection to Cursor*. It makes the selected Cube jump to the 3D Cursor location (Figure 2.22).

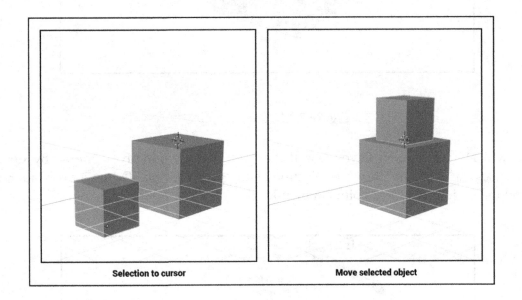

Figure 2.22 - Cubes after the Snap

Since our Cube's origin point is at the bottom, it will sit perfectly on top of the other object. You can use the same workflow to move and align other 3D models.

Tip: Always use the Snap to move and precisely align objects. The Snap also works in Edit Mode for elements like edges and faces.

2.5.1 Pivot points and transformations

The origin point can assume additional functions in object manipulation, like defining a pivot point for transformations like rotation and scaling. For instance, if you select an object with the origin point in its center, you will get a rotation from that pivot, and all scaling operations will either expand or shrink based on that point (Figure 2.23).

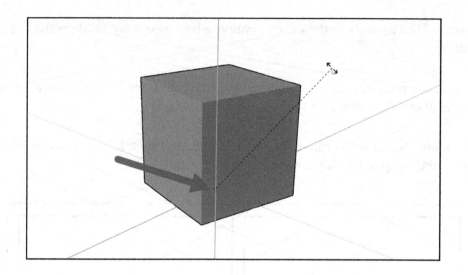

Figure 2.23 - Pivot example

That will always happen if you use the default settings for pivot points. By default, Blender uses the Median Point of a selection as the pivot. At the 3D Viewport header, you will find the options for pivot points in Blender (Figure 2.24).

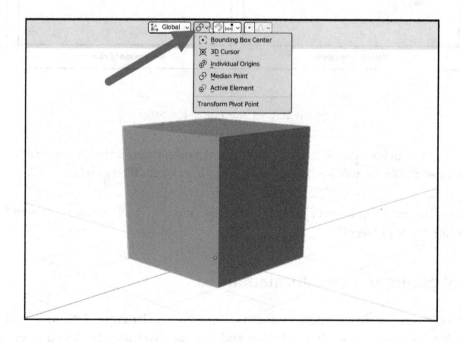

Figure 2.24 - Pivot options

There you can set different ways to handle pivot points:

- **Bounding Box Center**: You will use a cube projection shape based on all objects you have in a selection. The center of that projection will be the pivot point.

- **3D Cursor**: The 3D Cursor location will be your pivot point when you use this option.

- **Individual Origins**: When multiple objects are selected, you can use each origin point as a pivot. It is excellent to apply a rotation or scale to various objects as if they were single selections.

- **Median Point**: The default option uses an object origin point for single selections or the median point between multiple selected objects.

- **Active Element**: You can use the active object's origin as a pivot if you select various objects. The active object is always the last one selected.

Managing pivot points in Blender is an option that can save you a lot of time if used correctly. For instance, if you look at the model shown in Figure 2.25, you will see a chair. The origin point for that model is close to the object median location, which is not ideal for that type of 3D model.

Figure 2.25 - Chair model

Since the model usually aligns with the floor from the bottom, you should place the pivot point at the lowest point. Keeping the pivot point in any other location might add extra editing steps every time you scale or rotate the object.

Remember that in a scale transformation, you get the object contracting or expanding using the origin as a reference (Figure 2.26).

Figure 2.26 - Scale example

After applying a scale using a pivot located anywhere but the bottom, you must move the object and align your model with the floor again since the scale changes the size of each chair leg. Place the origin point at the bottom to avoid that extra editing step.

It will make the model scale up and down and keep the legs above the floor (Figure 2.27).

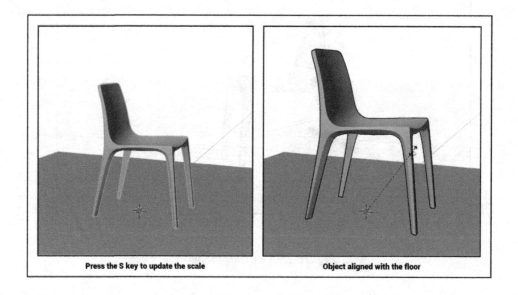

Press the S key to update the scale   Object aligned with the floor

Figure 2.27 - Scale using the bottom as pivot

You can either move the origin point to that location or align the 3D Cursor to the bottom vertices and change pivot settings to use that location. However, you should try to set the origin point of objects in a location where they might get an advantage in modeling tasks.

The best location for an object that should stay above a surface will always be the contact point between the model and a surface (Figure 2.28).

Figure 2.28 - Chair model

The chair model should have the origin point at the bottom because it is the most probable place you will use to align it with the floor.

Tip: *The origin point is the insertion location for objects you bring from external files using the Append or Link options. If you have plans to reuse a model, it is even more important to set the best possible origin point.*

2.6 Object collections

After you start creating objects, the 3D Viewport will become crowded with many 3D Models. In Blender, we can work with a tool called Collections that lets you create something similar to groups. By using Collections, you have much better control over complex scenes.

The Collections appear in the Outliner Editor in the top right of your default user interface (Figure 2.29).

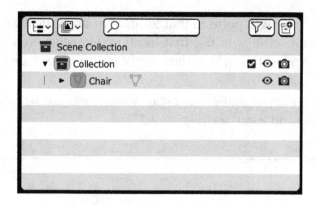

Figure 2.29 - *Outliner Editor*

At the Outliner, you have the Scene Collection, the base for all Blender files. Even if you don't want to use any new Collections, it appears as the base for your scene.

You also have a "Collection" with your default Cube, Camera, and Lamp. All objects you add to the scene will go to the Active Collection. You will see a small greyed circle next to the Collection name showing if it is active (Figure 2.30).

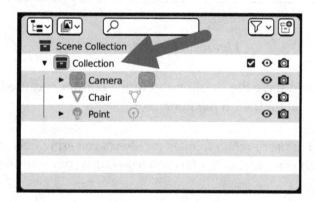

Figure 2.30 - *Active Collection*

To make a Collection active, you can click on their name.

Info: You will also see the active Collection name at the top left corner of your 3D Viewport.

You can create new Collections using several different options. In the Outliner Editor, right-click on a space and choose "New" to create a Collection (Figure 2.31).

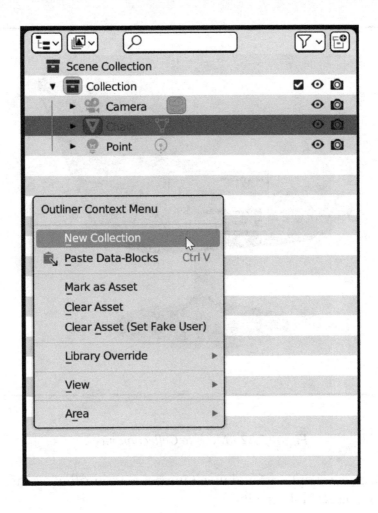

Figure 2.31 - New Collection

With a double-click on any Collection name, you can rename them to something that helps you manage the scene. Still, in the Outliner Editor, you can move objects between Collections with a simple drag and drop. It is even possible to drag and drop full Collections and nest them inside other Collections.

Another way to move and manage Collections is with a shortcut in the 3D Viewport. If you select one or multiple objects and press the M key. It opens a small menu that lets you move the objects to an existing Collection or create a new one (Figure 2.32).

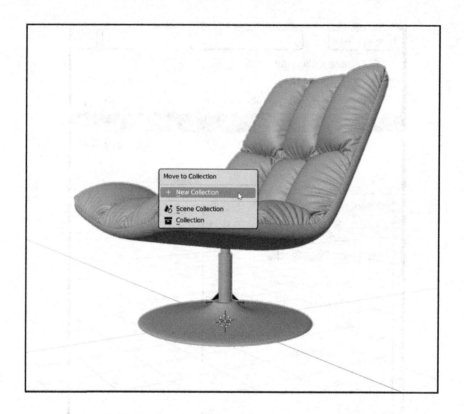

Figure 2.32 - Move to Collection menu

The use of Collections is optional and won't impact your creative results. But, using Collections might give you several benefits:

– You can put all objects from the same type in a single Collection. For instance, all furniture objects from a scene in a Collection are called furniture. That way, you can easily select all objects from a Collection using SHIFT+G.

– At the Collections controls, you can hide objects from a Collection from the 3D Viewport by clicking on the small eye icon. You can hide individual objects or the entire Collection.

– If you click on the eye icon while holding the CTRL key, you hide all other Collections but the one you are clicking. Click again to unhide.

– A Collection appears in the list of objects you can use to append from external files. Using the Append or Link options from the File menu will allow you to get all the contents of one or multiple Collections.

– There is an option to create instances of Collections using the SHIFT+A keys. Locate the Collection Instance option to add an instance of existing Collections.

As you can see from the list, you have multiple benefits from using Collections in your projects. Therefore, it is important to use them and assign meaningful names to each of the Collections. That helps to identify what types of objects they hold. Assign a unique name to a Collection also helps to identify the contents in a later Append or Link operation.

Tip: You can make copies of Collections from the Add menu. If you look at the bottom of the menu, you can create new instances from existing collections by pressing the SHIFT+A key.

2.6.1 Renaming objects

As you start to create objects in Blender, you will notice that their names appear as a combination of object type and a numeric sequence. The default Cube displays the name "Cube," after adding another object of the same kind, it receives the name "Cube.001".

Unless you rename those objects, after a few hours of work, you might have a scene filled with Cubes starting with "001" and going to "100". That is terrible for scene organization, and you will quickly lose control over the project.

Figure 2.33 - Object name selected

To avoid losing control, remember that each object in Blender must have a unique name.

To help manage object naming, you have multiple ways to identify the name of any selected object quickly. When you select an object, look at the top left corner. There you find the active Collection and the name of your selected object (Figure 2.33).

Assigning unique names to each object to keep the scene organized is a good practice. Setting names helps avoid having dozens, hundreds, or thousands of objects with default names followed by a number.

To rename an object, you can:

- **Select the object and press F2**: That calls a small menu that will let you pick a new name.

- **Double-click at the object name in the Outliner Editor**: You can rename the object straight from the Collections list.

- **Use the Properties Editor**: Select the object and go to the Object tab. At the top, you will be able to set a new name.

At the Properties Editor, you will have the object name at the top of that tab (Figure 2.34).

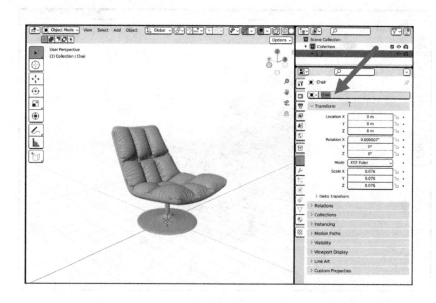

Figure 2.34 - *Properties Editor*

You should always assign names to your models to help you manage large scenes or bring objects from external files.

Tip: If you have objects with multiple parts, you can use the numeric suffix and place them all into a collection. Later you will be able to select or instance that Collection.

2.7 Using the Asset Browser

Until a couple of years ago, the easiest way to reuse models in Blender involved using either an Append or Link. The process is easy and straightforward and requires us to find the location and name of the asset you wish to use in a new project. After a few projects and accumulating many different assets, you will need help finding those models and assets.

For instance, if you have a chair model in a particular project that you want to use again for a new scene. To use the Append or Link, you must:

1. Know the Blender file name

2. Locate the file in your personal archives

3. Find the object name in the Blender file

Unless you have a separate control for your models, like a spreadsheet with file names and models, it will become hard to find a single model after accumulating many models.

To help solve this problem, we had the introduction in Blender of an editor called Asset Browser. With the Asset Browser, you can build a personal library of assets for quick reuse. It supports both 3D models and materials. The key to adding assets to this Editor is to prepare your projects with a special marking for each asset.

Once you start working on a project and think it might be helpful later, mark it as an asset. To do this, you can right-click on the object name and choose "Mark as Asset." In Figure 2.35, we have that option with a right-click in the Outliner Editor.

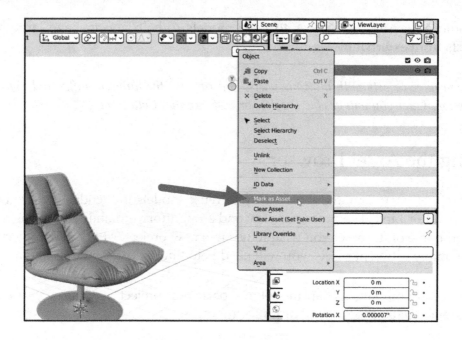

Figure 2.35 - *Mark object as an Asset*

Once you mark an object as an Asset, you see a small icon next to the object name. The icon of a stack of books identifies it as eligible for a library. It doesn't mean it goes automatically to a library because we need an extra step before it appears as a reusable resource. With that icon, the object is ready to join a library (Figure 2.36).

Figure 2.36 - *Asset icon*

By the way, we can unmark any object as an Asset with two options:

– Clear Asset

– Clear Asset (Fake User)

Those options appear when you right-click an object. With the first one, we remove the eligibility to become part of a library, and the second removes the "Mark" and adds a Fake User. The Fake User prevents Blender from purging that asset if it is not in the scene.

2.7.1 Creating a library

After setting the object or material as an Asset, we still have to do an extra step before using it in a library. It might seem simple, but we must save the Blender file somewhere. If you plan to start working with multiple libraries, I recommend using a dedicated folder for each group of files. For instance, we can save a Blender file with a chair model in an empty folder (Figure 2.37).

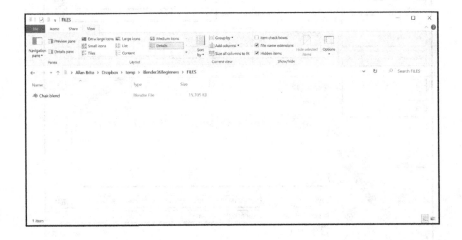

Figure 2.37 - Save the Blender file and place it in a unique folder

Notice that it is the only file in the folder. Remember that there is no problem saving a Blender file in a folder with dozens of other files. At some point, when you open the Asset Browser, Blender will have to read all files from that folder to identify models with the "Asset" mark. If you have dozens or hundreds of files, reading everything might require extra computational power and slow your system.

For that reason, it is always a great idea to keep Blender files used for the Asset Browser in a dedicated folder.

2.7.2 Using assets from the library

With a Blender file saved in a dedicated folder, we can create a Library for all files available from that location. That is a crucial step in using the Asset Browser. You can make as many libraries as needed from the Preferences Editor. Go to the **Edit → Preferences** menu and choose the File Paths tab.

You will see the "Asset Libraries" section with name and path options there. Click on the plus icon and create a new library. We can name this new library "Assets" and point the path to the same folder with the Blender file (Figure 2.38).

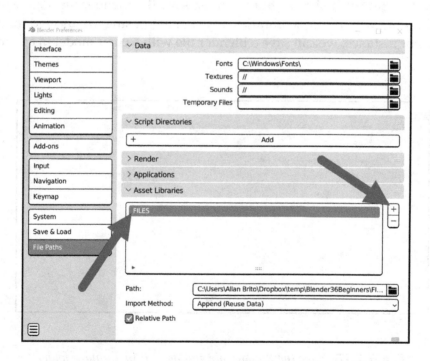

Figure 2.38 - Create the library and point select the folder

That is all we have to do in the preferences options. Once you have a name and a folder set as a library, Blender will try to read all files saved in that folder with data marked as an asset. You can now open the Asset Browser Editor (Figure 2.39).

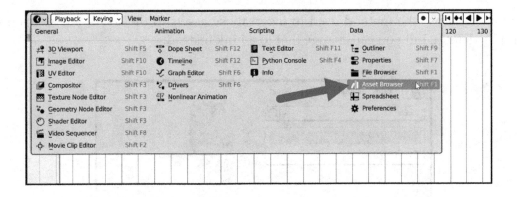

Figure 2.39 - *Open the Asset Browser*

How to select assets from the Asset Browser? All data appear in the Asset Browser based on the library you choose. Pick a library from the list available on the top-left of your Editor. After selecting a library by name, all available assets appear on the right (Figure 2.40).

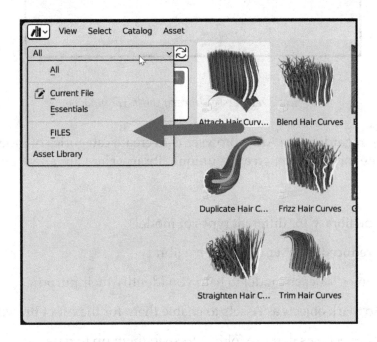

Figure 2.40 - *Library with Assets*

To add those models or materials to a new project, you can click and drag them to a scene (Figure 2.41). It is straightforward to use those assets. Notice that at the top, we also have the option to choose the method used to insert those assets in the scene. All assets use an Append by default, but you can change that to a Link instead.

Figure 2.41 - *Asset library with 3D models*

A good practice regarding the Asset Browser is to create categories of models and materials. From each category, you can create a unique library. Here are a few guidelines for the Asset Browser:

– Create a unique library for different types of models

– Try to keep a reduced number of assets in a library

– Use unique names for each model to help you identify their purpose

– Don't forget to mark objects as Assets to enable them for the Asset Browser

– You can save project files in those folders to keep them up to date

The Asset Browser is an incredible resource that saves time during project development. With time and planning, you will reduce your production time in Blender by reusing assets.

What is next?

Drawing Chapter 2 to a close, you've paved a solid foundation in the realm of 3D modeling with Blender. Delving into Edit Mode allowed you to sculpt and redefine 3D objects, while mastering transformations enabled you to maneuver and reshape Mesh structures utilizing vertices, edges, and faces. Your proficiency also extends to categorizing 3D objects within Collections and integrating them into external libraries for efficient access via the Asset Browser.

Imagine these tools as your digital chisel and marble—though foundational, they set the stage for boundless creation. Repeated practice hones these skills, ensuring your capacity to mold any envisioned 3D structure. Revisit this chapter periodically, especially to cement shortcuts in memory.

Chapter 3 awaits with a treasury of advanced 3D modeling tools. Ever stumbled upon the term 'extrude' in the 3D lexicon? Prepare to harness its transformative power, morphing 2D silhouettes into voluminous entities. Renowned as a linchpin of 3D modeling, the extrude function graces virtually every 3D software suite. Alongside it, we'll embark on lessons in edge loop management, shape bifurcation, vertex merging, and more.

Chapter 3 - Tools for 3D Modeling

Having grasped the basics of creating and modifying 3D objects in Blender, our journey now delves into advanced tools that transform these objects. Just as a painter learns the nuances of each brush, you'll be familiarizing yourself with key tools that shape 3D primitives —be it cubes, cylinders, or others—into desired designs. Chapters 3 and 4 introduce you to Blender's foundational tools for three-dimensional modeling.

A crucial Blender feature awaiting introduction is shading in the 3D Viewport. This feature not only refines how objects appear in the Viewport for easier modeling but also incorporates the X-Ray view mode, making opaque surfaces transparent.

Though we've touched on several vital subjects in the first few chapters, I must emphasize the unparalleled significance of the extrude tool. Foundational to all 3D production stages, Blender's extrude tool is versatile across various object types. As we navigate the chapters, you'll see its application in sculpting myriad shapes. Remember, the concept of extrusion isn't exclusive to Blender but is a staple in all 3D software.

We'll then venture into supplementary editing tools to augment 3D models in Blender, such as handling edge loops and employing the Loop Cut. Additionally, you'll learn to streamline objects by discarding superfluous vertices and dividing objects. Concluding the chapter, we illuminate the process of crafting symmetrical designs using the Mirror tool.

Here's a summary of what you will learn:

- Navigating through X-Ray and shading modes for a fresh perspective on your models.

- Mastering extrusion in polygon modeling and understanding various extrude modes.

- The intricate process of loop cutting and creating new edges and faces from vertices.

- Essential skills of separating and joining models in your project.

- Understanding the importance of merging vertices and its role in creating efficient models.

- Leveraging the Mirror tool for creating symmetrical models with ease.

3.1 X-Ray and shading modes for Modeling

As you start handling 3D objects in Blender for modeling tasks, using a tool called X-Ray to make your selections easier in those contexts will become critical. Why is X-Ray mode important for modeling? The mode helps you select and edit certain parts of objects occluded by existing geometry.

For instance, if you get a simple Cube in your 3D Viewport and try to select the bottom vertices using the B Key, you will notice that only the visible vertices become selected. You can easily select all vertices—even those behind existing faces using X-Ray mode.

Figure 3.1 - X-Ray Mode

To enable X-Ray Mode, use the button at the 3D Viewport header on the left of the shading modes (Figure 3.1).

Once you enable X-Ray Mode, you see all faces in 3D models as semi-transparent surfaces. As they become transparent, you will select those elements using tools like the B Key (Figure 3.2).

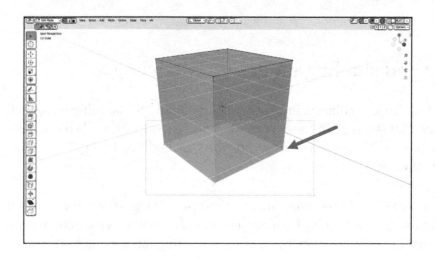

Figure 3.2 - *Using a box selection*

Enabling X-Ray mode allows you to remain in a shading mode like Solid and still select and interact with elements of your model behind faces.

3.1.1 Shading modes

If you don't want to use X-Ray to visualize elements occluded by your 3D model's surfaces, you can swap between shading modes to help with a challenging selection. Even being a subject related to rendering, you can use those modes to make your modeling tasks easier.

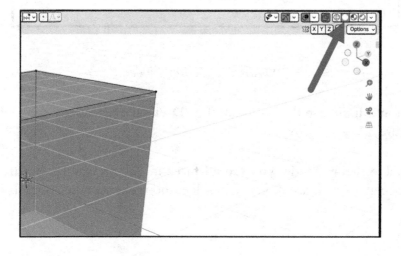

Figure 3.3 - *Shading modes*

Shading modes are available on the right side of your 3D Viewport header (Figure 3.3). You can also use the Z key to change those modes quickly.

There you can choose from four main shading modes:

– **Wireframe**: A simple mode where you will see your models' polygon structure using only the lines connecting the vertices.

– **Solid**: The default mode for shading is viewing models with a solid color for all faces.

– **Material Preview**: Here, we have a mode that shows a simplified version of your lights and displays materials for surfaces.

– **Rendered**: The most advanced mode where you will view shadows, textures, and lights.

It is possible to work in a Rendered mode for your projects, which gives real-time updates on lights and materials. Still, you might experience some performance issues depending on your scene's complexity and the available hardware (Figure 3.4).

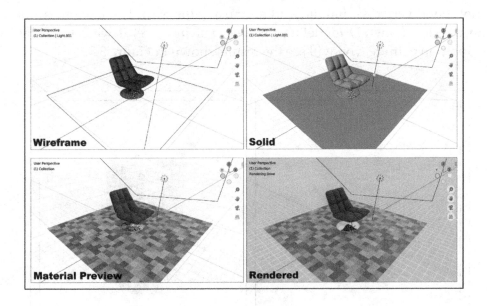

Figure 3.4 - Shading modes

For modeling projects, the best approach is to stay between Wireframe and Solid. They offer the best combination of performance and visualization options for your projects. Even in Wireframe mode, you still might have occluded elements based on the location and viewing angle.

Whenever parts of a 3D model are occluded by existing geometry, enable X-Ray mode to select those parts regardless of your viewing angle.

3.2 Extrude for polygon modeling

A geometrical primitive like a Cube or Cylinder in a scene could be great for learning purposes, but you will probably want to modify their shapes to build different objects. Regarding object transformation and modeling, you will find that one option in Blender is among the most used tools for polygon modeling.

The extrude is a tool that allows us to select and expand the shape of a Mesh object. To start an extrude, you always begin selecting a vertex, edge, or face. With the extrude, you get a copy of the selected elements connected to the original parts. That is a simple way to describe how it works.

It may not sound very clear initially, but after using the extrude a few times, you will see how it can transform any 3D modeling pipeline. For instance, if we select a face from a Cube and apply an extrude, you will see the results shown in Figure 3.5.

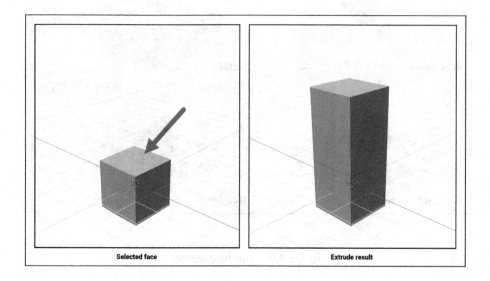

Figure 3.5 - *Extrude applied to face*

You can also apply an extrude to either a vertex or edge. For a vertex, you will get an edge as a result, and if you select an edge, it creates a plane (Figure 3.6).

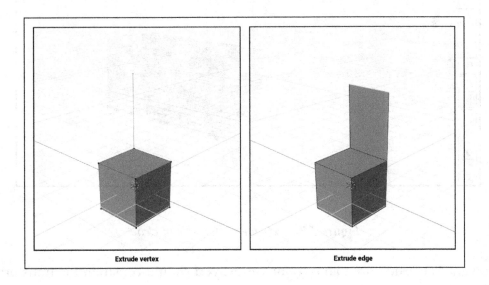

Figure 3.6 - Extrude in vertices and edges

How to use the extrude? The easiest way to trigger an extrude is with the E key in Edit Mode. The shortcut calls the Extrude Region option. After selecting the target elements, you want to extrude, press the E key to start.

If you perform the extrude entirely with the mouse, you must left-click somewhere to end the transformation. That gives you only visual feedback on the length of your resulting shape.

Like the move transformation learned in Chapter 2, you can assign numeric values to each extrude. For instance, if you want to create an extruded face with two units in size:

1. Select the face

2. Press the E key

3. Type 2

4. Press RETURN to confirm

All extrudes from faces occur perpendicularly from the selected face (Figure 3.7).

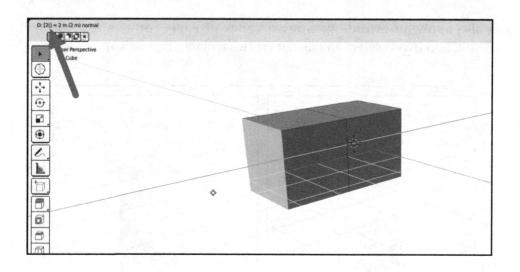

Figure 3.7 - *Extrude with a size of two*

If you want to extrude from an edge or vertex, you should constrain the transformation to an axis.

3.2.1 Extrude modes

Besides the E key, you can also trigger the extrude using the options from the Toolbar. There you will find four buttons with different types of extrudes (Figure 3.8).

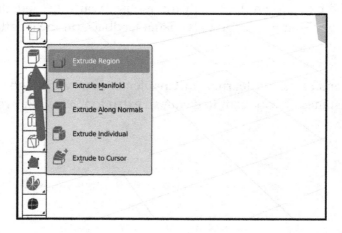

Figure 3.8 - *Extrude in the Toolbar*

Here are all the extrude types:

- **Extrude Region**: Select one or multiple elements to extrude them as a single block. That is the default extrude option you can trigger with the E key.

- **Extrude Manifold**: A powerful new extrude mode introduced with Blender 2.9 that can automatically divide and erase faces based on their location. It is a great tool to extrude the interior of your existing model.

- **Extrude Along Normals**: The extrude will use the element normals to get a direction. Usually, the normals go toward the perpendicular direction from the selected element.

- **Extrude Individual**: You can create an extrude from multiple elements like you selected each one individually. The extrudes will go in a unique direction for each selected element.

- **Extrude to Cursor**: The extrude will go to the mouse cursor location. It will create irregular shapes depending on the cursor position on the screen

You can also call different extrudes with the ALT+E key that brings the Extrude menu to the screen (Figure 3.9).

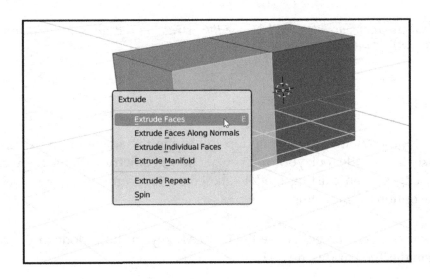

Figure 3.9 - *Extrude menu*

Sometimes, you will also see the contextual menu when you create objects in the 3D Viewport. You can change values for your extrude's offset (length) (Figure 3.10).

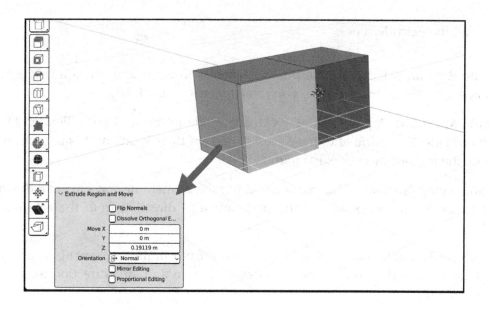

Figure 3.10 - *Contextual menu for extrudes*

Remember that using the contextual menu is only possible after you finish the extrude. It works the same way as with object creation. If you start another operation in Blender, you can no longer change settings using that menu. That is because Blender is not parametrical.

Tip: The Toolbar options are also available for the extrude in a floating menu that you can open using the SHIFT+SPACEBAR keys.

3.3 Loop cut

The Loop cut tool is another helpful option to change the shape of an existing object in Blender. Unlike the extrude tool, you won't create new geometry with the Loop cut. Instead, you add new edges to an existing model—the edges loop around your model's shape to give you more options in modeling.

To use a Loop cut, you can either use the CTRL+R keys in Edit Mode or the corresponding button from the Toolbar (Figure 3.11).

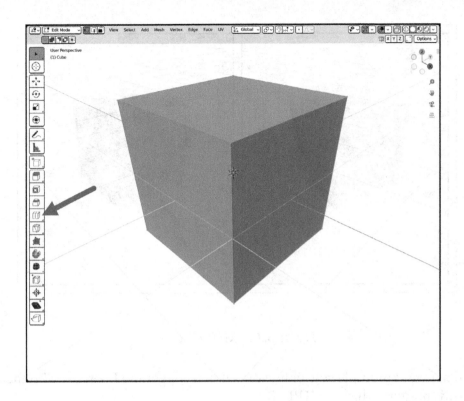

Figure 3.11 - *Loop cut button*

After pressing either the shortcut key or the button, you have to use a small sequence of clicks to create and align the Loop cut:

1. Move the mouse cursor over an edge. The cut will occur in a perpendicular direction from that edge.

2. Left-click once to confirm the direction of the cut

3. Move the cursor again to choose the location of your edge loop

4. Left-click again to set the location

5. To make your new Loop stay in the middle, you can press the ESC key instead of left-clicking

You can also create multiple cuts with the Loop cut while still selecting your new loops' direction. Before confirming the direction of your cuts with the first left click, you can use the mouse wheel or the plus and minus keys from your Numpad to create multiple cuts (Figure 3.12).

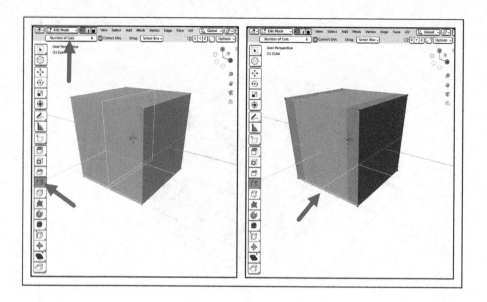

Figure 3.12 - *Multiple cuts*

That option to add multiple cuts only works if you trigger the Loop cut with their respective keyboard shortcut, which is CTRL+R.

After you add edge loops to the model, you can select the faces or any other element to apply an extrude. That gives you a lot of freedom regarding 3D modeling. It is possible to edit the number of cuts after adding them with the "Loop Cut and Slide" menu on the lower right corner of the 3D Viewport. Use the "Number of Cuts" to edit your Loop cut.

3.3.1 Loop cut and Extrude Manifold

A powerful option introduced recently is the Extrude Manifold, which can erase and split faces based on extrudes. It works better for extrudes made to the interior of a model. You can see the real benefit of such extrude when pairing it with a Loop cut.

To see the benefits of such extrude, we can take an example from a simple cube that receives a horizontal segment with the Loop cut. After you segment the cube, press the ALT+E keys and select Extrude Manifold (Figure 3.13).

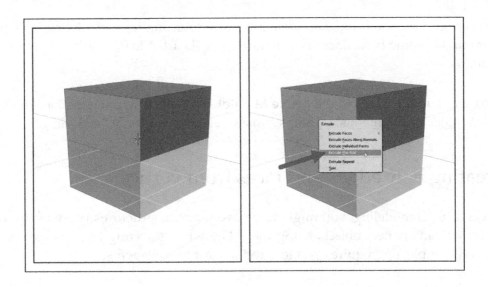

Figure 3.13 - *Cube with single cut*

In Figure 3.14, you can see a selected face where we apply both an Extrude Region and a Manifold.

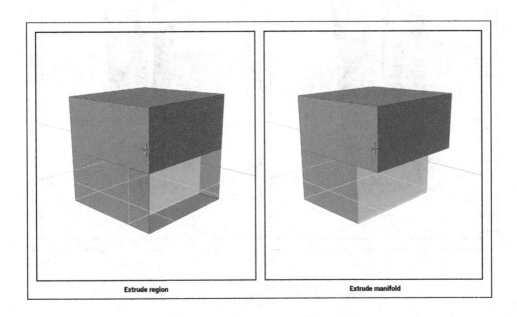

Figure 3.14 - *Comparing extrudes*

As you can see from the comparison, we got a face resulting from our Extrude Region going inward and keeping both sides. That requires the 3D artist to do additional work to "fix" the geometry.

On the other hand, we have the Extrude Manifold managing to push the face inward and editing both sides simultaneously. That is a massive timesaver for 3D modeling.

3.4 Creating new edges and faces from vertices

In some cases in 3D modeling, you might have two separate structures you wish to connect. In Blender, we can connect objects using the F key when selecting two vertices or edges. The process is simple and requires you to select at least two elements.

Select two vertices in a model in Edit Mode and press the F key to connect them with an edge (Figure 3.15).

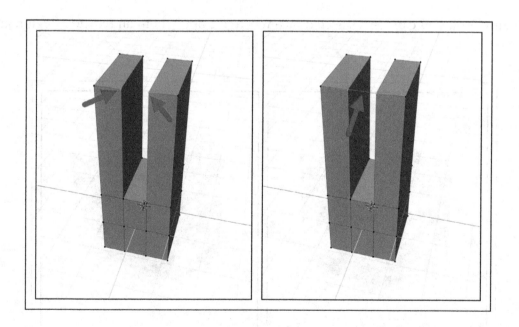

Figure 3.15 - Connecting vertices

You can also connect three and four vertices resulting in a face. Selecting three vertices also creates a new face. However, it is a common practice to avoid such types of faces. A triangular face usually breaks edge loops and won't create smooth deformations in animations.

If you select two edges, you can press the F key to connect them with a face (Figure 3.16).

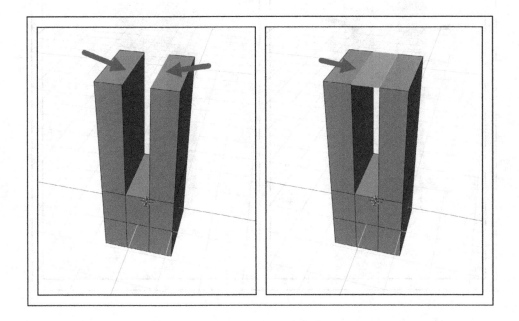

Figure 3.16 - *Connecting two edges*

The F key is a great tool to create new geometry based on connections of elements from a Mesh.

3.4.1 Connecting faces with the Bridge faces

The F key can connect the vertices and edges of a model but won't work when the selected element is a face. To connect faces in a model, we have to use another tool. We need the *Bridge Faces* that appear in the Context Menu for faces. After selecting two faces, right-click to open that menu (Figure 3.17).

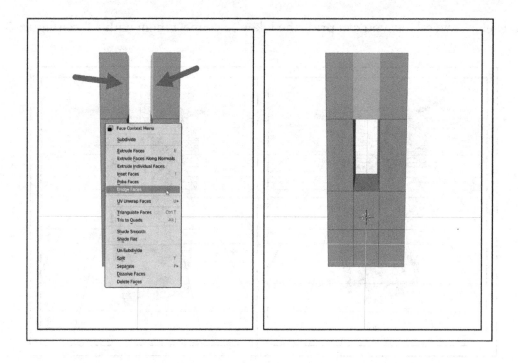

Figure 3.17 - *Context menu and Bridge Faces*

With the Bridge Faces, it is possible to connect two selected faces and create new geometry. You have to select the faces first and press the right mouse button. That opens the Context Menu. Pick Bridge Faces, and you get a connection between the two selected faces.

The option will only work if you have up to two faces selected. With Bridge Faces, you get better results by using parallel faces. That is a way to avoid distorted shapes from the connected geometry.

3.5 Separating and joining models

In the previous section, we learned how to connect elements from a model with the F key and the Bridge Faces. What if we want to separate models instead of joining them?

To separate parts of a model in Blender, use the P key. After pressing the P key, a small menu appears with options. It is possible to separate parts by selection, materials, and loose parts.

For instance, after pressing the P key and choosing "Selection," Blender creates a new object based on any selected vertices, edges, or faces. The separate option is helpful for projects where you must create derivate models from existing 3D objects. An isolated part could work as a starting point for new 3D models.

For example, look at the model shown in Figure 3.18.

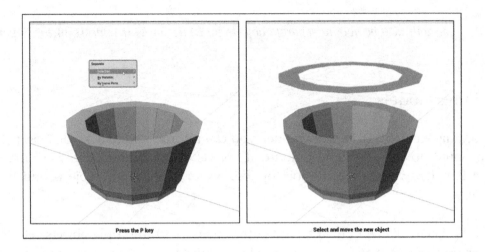

Figure 3.18 - *Separate sequence and results*

This model aims to start a derivate object using the faces pointed out in Figure 3.18 *(Left)*. It already has the correct size and scale. To create a new model based on that selection, use the following workflow:

1. Make sure you have the correct faces selected

2. Press SHIFT+D to duplicate the faces

3. Press the ESC key to cancel the transformation of your duplicated faces

4. With the duplicated faces still selected, press the P key

5. Choose "Selection"

6. Switch to Object Mode

After switching to Object Mode, a new object based on those faces will be available for you to start modeling. If you can't select the new object, look at the Collections for a duplicate.

The technique consists of canceling the transformation for the duplicated object with the ESC key. That creates new objects in the same location as the initially selected faces. It also works for copies of edges and vertices. However, in Figure 3.18 *(Right)*, the new object is in a higher Z coordinate to make it easier to visualize the outcome.

There is also an option in the **Mesh → Separate** menu to call the Separate options without the shortcut key.

Tip: Later, you will also be able to separate objects by Material as it appears in the Separate options.

3.5.1 Joining models

After separating elements from a 3D model, you can return them to a single object. That requires an option to turn multiple individual objects into a unified entity. To merge two meshes in Blender, we can use the Join option. Select two or more objects and press the CTRL+J keys.

The join is also available in the **Object → Join** menu with multiple objects selected. Unlike the Separate option that required you to be in Edit Mode, you must trigger the Join option in Object Mode.

Using the Join option is useful when connecting parts of two different objects. The F key won't work on two separate objects, and also the Bridge Faces. With the Join tool, you can easily make a new object based on two or more shapes.

If you don't want to keep models as a single object, you can do all modeling tasks and separate them again with the P key.

3.6 Merging vertices

A typical modeling project in Blender might require a few hours of work using tools to extrude, connect, and cut models. That work results in a 3D object ready to receive materials and textures for rendering. It is possible to end up with duplicated vertices, edges or faces in a particular region during the process.

That could create visual problems with modifiers like Subdivision Surface. In 3D modeling, those visual problems usually receive the name of "artifacts."

Luckily, we have a quick way to eliminate those duplicates using an option from the *Context Menu* called *Merge*. Using the Merge option, you can get two or more vertices from a model and turn them into a single vertex.

Info: The Merge options only appear when you have Vertex marked as the primary selection in Edit Mode.

For instance, in Figure 3.19, you see a model with two vertices that we could merge.

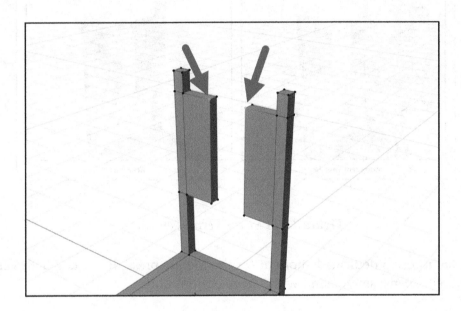

Figure 3.19 - Vertices for Merge

To use all options regarding merging, you can use the Context Menu in edit mode. Select the elements and right-click once. In the list, you will see the following options:

— **At First or At Last**: Use the first or last selected vertex.

— **At Center**: All vertices will merge using the median distance between them.

— **At Cursor**: The new vertex created will use the 3D Cursor location.

— **Collapse**: You will get islands of vertices merged based on the distance between them. Each island will merge into a new vertex.

— **By distance**: You will merge vertices based on the distance between them. For instance, zero length will remove all duplicated vertices from a 3D model.

For the vertices from Figure 3.19, we can quickly fix the gap between those two vertices with a Merge based on the median distance. Select both vertices and with a right-click, call the Context menu and pick **Merge → At Center** (Figure 3.20).

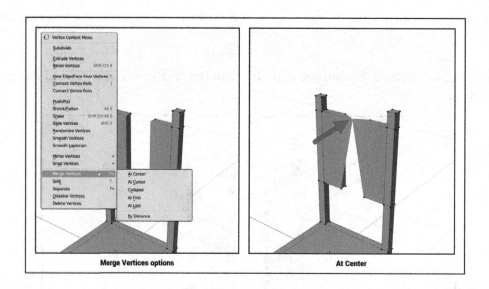

Figure 3.20 - *Merge Vertices options*

If you want to use a dedicated shortcut for the Merge, press the M key with vertices selected. That will open a small menu with Merge options only.

Tip: *For the example in Figure 3.20, you can repeat the Merge to connect the other vertices.*

3.6.1 Fixing extrudes with the Merge

One of the uses for the Merge option in Blender is to fix problems created by the extrude, where you might forget to undo a canceled extrude during the transformation stage.

The problem appears when you press the E key to extrude and the ESC key before finishing the extrude. That cancels the transformation, but the extruded's new elements will still exist in your scene.

By pressing CTRL+Z right after that operation, you remove those extra elements (vertices, edges, or faces). But, if you forget to press CTRL+Z or use the **Edit → Undo** menu, all newly created elements will stay present until you see visual problems from modifiers and other operations.

You can quickly fix that problem with a Merge using the distance option. Look at Figure 3.21 *(Left)* for a model with a canceled extrude for one of their faces.

Visually, the model doesn't have anything wrong with the polygon structure. But, if you select all vertices and press the M key (Merge) and choose the "By Distance" option, you will see a message in the status bar of Blender pointing that it removed 12 vertices (Figure 3.21).

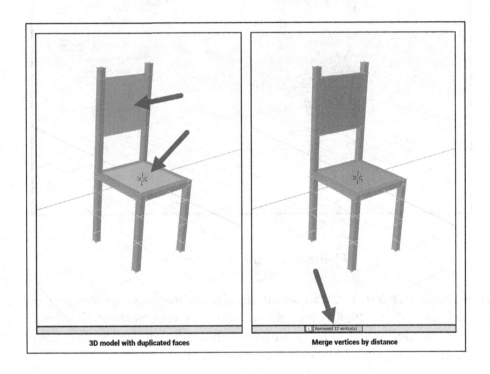

3D model with duplicated faces   Merge vertices by distance

Figure 3.21 - Removed duplicated vertices

The downside of this procedure is that you must trigger the Merge option to remove duplicates manually.

But, an option from the Sidebar of Blender allows you to enable an *Auto Merge* option that automatically removes duplicates. Open the Sidebar with the N key and go to the Tools tab (Figure 3.22).

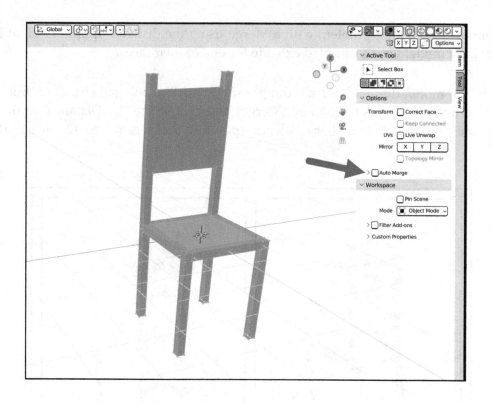

Figure 3.22 - *Auto Merge option*

With *Auto Merge* enabled, you can set the minimum distance for merging polygon elements. The default distance (0.001) will ensure you have only vertices sharing the same location receiving an *Auto Merge*. Leave *Auto Merge* enabled to make Blender remove all those vertices without pressing the M key or the Context Menu.

3.7 Using the Mirror Tool for Modeling

Many objects subject to 3D modeling in Blender will present some symmetry. Working with any object with a symmetrical side makes your life a lot easier because we can create only half of the shape and mirror the other side.

In Blender, you have a few options to work with symmetrical models starting with the Mirror tool and going up until the Mirror Modifier used in Chapter 4.

The Mirror tool in Blender works with the CTRL+M key, which inverts any selected objects. You won't get a mirrored copy with the tool but an inverted model version. For instance, we can take the model shown in Figure 3.23 *(Left)*, representing only half of a 3D object.

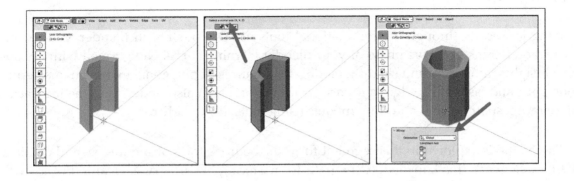

Figure 3.23 - Half of a model to use with the Mirror

If you go to Object Mode, press CTRL+M, or use the **Object → Mirror** menu, you can invert the object shape. For the shortcut, you must press a key representing the axis in which the mirror will happen (Figure 3.23 - *Middle*). Press the key corresponding to an axis after the CTRL+M.

By choosing the **Object → Mirror** menu, you can pick the axis you want to use from the options list. The result will be a flipped version of the model. Using a SHIFT+D before you make the mirror, it is possible to create an inverted version of the model using a duplicate.

Using a move transformation with the flipped duplicate makes it possible to create a full model with perfect symmetry (Figure 3.23 - *Right*). Since they will be different objects, use a CTRL+J to join them, and later apply a Merge using the distance option. It removes all duplicated vertices and weld the parts as a single object.

Tip: A trick some artists use to apply a mirror using the Scale transformation consists of a scale with -100% of the object size. For instance, select the object and press the S key. Type -1 as the factor to get a mirror image of that model.

What is next?

Having journeyed through the foundational tools of 3D modeling in Blender, you've embarked on a transformative phase of your Blender learning curve. Now armed with invaluable insights into X-Ray and shading modes, the nuances of polygonal extrusion, mastering loop cuts, and fashioning edges and faces from vertices, you also understand the intricacies of merging, splitting, and reflecting models using tools like the Mirror.

The methods explored in this segment form the bedrock for crafting lifelike and detailed 3D models. With this knowledge, the path to mastering 3D artistry is clearer. But as with any craft, perfection demands practice, so don't hesitate to tinker and revisit this chapter for clarity.

Up next in Chapter 4, brace yourself for an elevation in your modeling prowess. Aptly named 'Modeling Techniques and Resources,' it unlocks the enchanting realm of 'Modifiers for modeling.' Modifiers, powerful in their essence, promise finesse to your models in mere clicks.

As the expansive universe of 3D modeling in Blender unfurls, cherish every step, absorb every lesson, and let your creative spirit soar. Onward to Chapter Four!

Chapter 4 - Modeling Techniques and Resources

In the previous chapter, we introduced the essential tools and features Blender offers to craft versatile 3D models. This chapter broadens our toolkit, delving deeper into Blender's array of features that grant you increased creative control. We're about to explore modifiers and harness their full potential in 3D modeling.

Chapter 4 kicks off with a breakdown of the purpose and significance of modifiers in the realm of 3D modeling, as well as guidance on how to organize and layer them for diverse effects. Through modifiers, you can dramatically transform the visual essence of a 3D object, bestowing it with a distinctive flair.

Prominent among these modifiers is the Subdivision Surface, a favorite tool among professionals to produce intricately detailed 3D models. By employing this modifier, even a simple model can be enriched with smoother surfaces and additional facets—all at the click of a button. To novices in 3D modeling, the results might appear almost magical.

The chapter will later cover two pivotal modifiers used for boolean operations. The Boolean modifier facilitates the crafting of 3D shapes through basic operations like subtraction, union, and intersection. Moreover, the Mirror modifier enables real-time symmetrical design for any 3D object.

Here's a summary of what you will learn:

– Leveraging the power of Modifiers for modeling.

– Mastering the Subdivision Surface modifier to create smooth, organic shapes.

– Exploring the potential of the Mirror and Array modifiers.

– Learning how to create complex shapes with the Boolean modifier.

– Using the Spin tool for creating rounded shapes.

– Understanding and utilizing Proportional editing for precise modifications.

4.1 Modifiers for modeling

In Blender, you'll encounter an extensive array of tools tailored for modeling, each beneficial in diverse project scenarios. Some of these tools stand out for their adaptability in modeling processes, as they provide a straightforward method to toggle specific workflow
facets on and off.

Among these standout tools are the modifiers. You can access modifiers from the Properties Editor, specifically under the Modifiers tab (as seen in Figure 4.1).

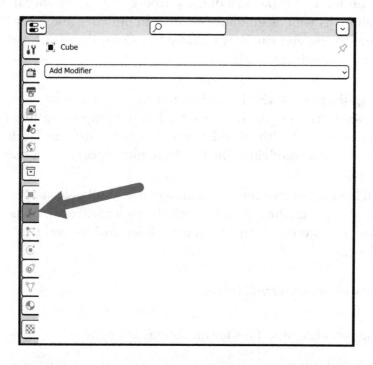

Figure 4.1 - *Modifier tab in the Properties Editor*

While modifiers are versatile and can be instrumental in varied contexts, not just modeling, our initial focus will be on leveraging them to reshape our 3D objects. To embark on
this transformative journey, begin by selecting an object you'd like to "modify."

Use the "Add Modifier" option to pick one or more modifiers from the list. Once you add
a modifier to an object, it appears in the Properties Editor in the Modifier tab (Figure 4.2).

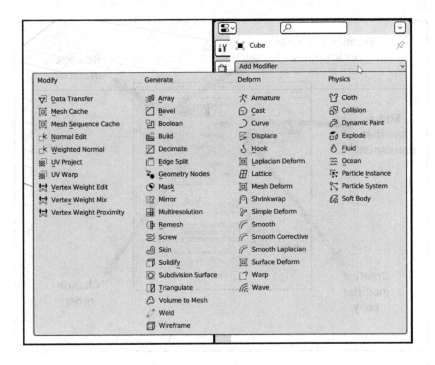

Figure 4.2 - *Modifier list*

A few aspects of modifiers that you should keep in mind:

– You can add as many modifiers to an object as you wish.

– The modifiers will stack on top of each other.

– Modifiers transform the model following the order in which they appear in the stack. Starting with the top modifier and following the order until the bottom.

– At any moment, you can reorder or remove a modifier from an object to exclude any modification made by that modifier.

Each modifier displays a few common controls to manage stack order, modifier duplication, make the modifier permanent, and more.

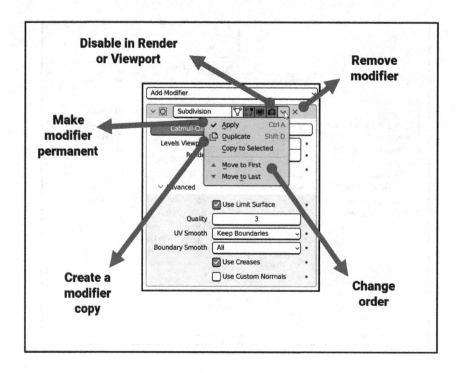

Figure 4.3 - *Modifier controls*

To view all controls, press the small button (arrow pointing down) on the top right, next to the camera button. In Figure 4.3, you can see a list of available controls.

An essential aspect of each modifier is that you will lose any effects it produces once you remove them from any object. You can use an "Apply" option to make the modifier effects permanent. After using that option, the modifier disappears from the list, and the modification becomes part of the object.

That is useful when you have a project where you must create an object based on multiple modifiers, which you can also use as a reference to start modeling. For instance, it is possible to add a Mirror Modifier and make it a permanent part of a 3D model.

Tip: *Before applying a modifier's, you should make a backup copy of your 3D model and place it in a different Collection. Create a copy of the model that has modifiers. That way, you can always go back to the original shape if you decide to start over the modeling process. By hiding that Collection, you keep an untouched version of any 3D model with all modifiers.*

4.2 Subdivision Surface modifier

One of the most used modifiers for modeling is the Subdivision Surface, which smoothes your 3D models by adding many new faces to the selected polygon. The modifier is one of the primary tools for techniques such as mesh modeling.

A popular workflow for many modeling projects is to start with a low poly version of an object and later apply a modification to increase polygon count. By adding more polygons, it is also possible to smooth existing surfaces.

Figure 4.4 shows an example of Subdivision Surface Modifier (High Poly) results.

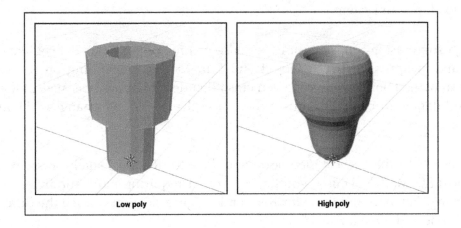

Figure 4.4 - Smoothing 3D model

To use that modifier, select the object you wish to smooth and pick Subdivision Surface from the modifier list. After assigning the modifier, it is possible to control smoothness from the modifier options (Figure 4.5).

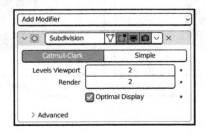

Figure 4.5 - Subdivision settings

What will determine the smoothness of your model is a combination of the subdivision count and algorithm. At the top, you will see two smoothing algorithms:

– **Catmull-Clark**: If you want a complete smoothing of your model with rounded shapes, use this method.

– **Simple**: You can use the simple option for projects where you want only new faces and divisions but no smoothing.

The level of subdivisions shows unique values for smoothing objects in the Viewport and Render. Usually, you will use a lower value for the Viewport and a higher level for the Render. The reason is that a model with a high level of subdivisions may add a significant computational load to your system.

With high subdivisions, you might experience common operations delays like changing the zoom and swapping between Object and Edit Modes. Depending on the value and number of smoothed objects, you can even crash Blender. It happens because of the amount of detail and data your computer must process to calculate simple changes, like refreshing the viewport.

A value of two for the "Levels Viewport" and three for Render usually show excellent results for most 3D Models. Unless you have a project requiring more subdivisions, always use two for the Viewport and three for Render. In Figure 4.6, you can see the difference between using one and three for subdivisions.

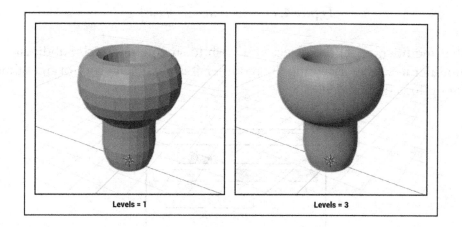

Figure 4.6 - Different levels of subdivision

With the Quality value, you can control the accuracy of how your modifier will place the vertices concerning the original object. Higher values result in improved precision for subdivisions, but add more computational load to the model.

4.2.1 Controlling surface smoothing

Even after using the Subdivision Surface modifier in a model, you might still see a few faces showing up. The modifier helps create a smooth surface for the model but won't remove visible borders from its faces.

To smooth the surface of any model, we have two shading options:

– Shade Smooth

– Shade Flat

By default, all models use Shade Flat, and in case you want to remove visible borders between polygons, change it to Shade Smooth. The option is available when you are in Object Mode. With an object selected, right-click to open the Context menu (Figure 4.7 - *Right*).

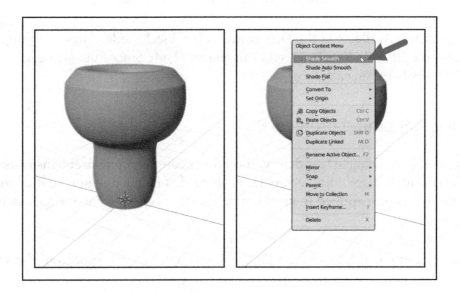

Figure 4.7 - *Context menu - Shade options*

There you will see the Shading options, and by choosing Shade Smooth, you remove the visible borders between each face (Figure 4.8).

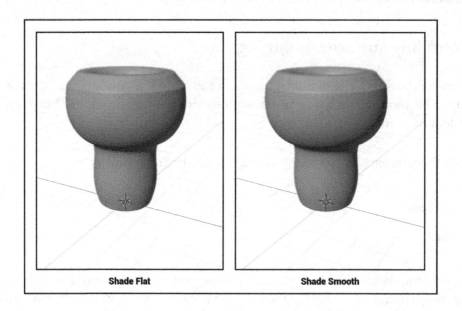

Figure 4.8 - *Results of a Shade Smooth*

The option is also available at the **Object** Menu in Object Mode. After assigning a Subdivision Surface modifier to any object, you can enable Shade Smooth to create a surface with no visible borders between each face.

4.2.2 Fixing smoothing problems

In the process of smoothing 3D models, you might encounter a few problems caused by unmatched face normals. Face normals are the visible side of a 3D polygon, and depending on the tools and techniques applied to create each object, you may have normals facing in opposite directions.

For instance, looking at the object in Figure 4.9, you see a dark spot from the smoothing process.

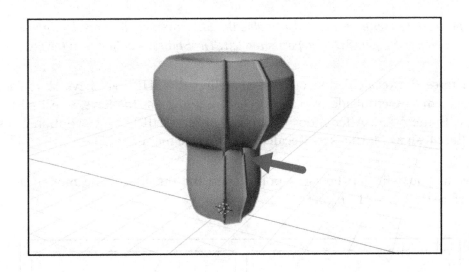

Figure 4.9 - Object with dark spot

To view the difference between normals in that object, we can enable the visualization of Face normals in the Overlays menu (*Edit Mode*). That menu is available on the left of your shading options at the 3D Viewport header (Figure 4.10).

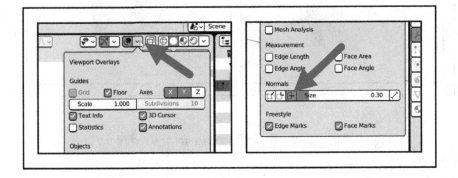

Figure 4.10 - Overlay options

Look to the lower side of your Overlays menu to find all options related to Normals. Enable the option to display normals for faces and increase their size. The normals appear as small perpendicular lines pointing out of each face.

You must be in Edit Mode to view and manipulate Normals. As you can see from Figure 4.11 (*Left*), the normals for part of the object point in opposite directions. If you want a smooth surface for any object, all normals must point in the same direction.

You can force the recalculation of normals using the SHIFT+N keys to make Blender point all of them to the outside of a model. Before you press the keys, select all faces from the object with the A key. After choosing all faces, press SHIFT+N. The option is also available from the **Mesh → Normals → Recalculate Outside** menu.

As a result, you will get the faces pointing to the outside of the model and a clean, smooth surface (Figure 4.11 - *Right*).

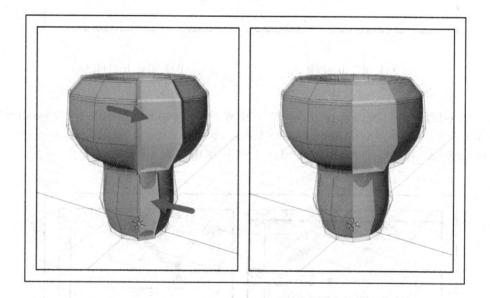

Figure 4.11 - *Clean smooth surface with fixed Normals*

Whenever you see dark spots on an object surface after applying a Subdivision Surface modifier and a Shade Smooth, you probably have an issue with Face normals. Enable the display of Face normals in the Overlays menu to investigate and apply a fix.

You have additional options to handle normals in the **Mesh → Normals** menu.

Tip: If you want to invert the normals of a face, you can use the Flip option from the Mesh → Normals menu.

4.2.3 Controlling smoothing radius with loops

Once you apply a Subdivision Surface modifier to an object, you will notice that it rounds the edges and corners for those 3D models. It is possible to control the roundness based on the distance between each edge of a mesh. You can control the smoothness radius with the Loop cut tool.

We can visually set the radius length by adding new edge loops close to the existing edges. For instance, if we add a new loop near the top of a model with the CTRL+R key and place it close to the upper edges. As a result, you get a smooth effect with a reduced radius.

If you look at the model shown in Figure 4.12, you will see that it uses a sizeable relative radius for the smoothed version, which is the left part of the image. To control the smoothness, we can add a new edge loop or cut. Move that new loop near the top to reduce your radius.

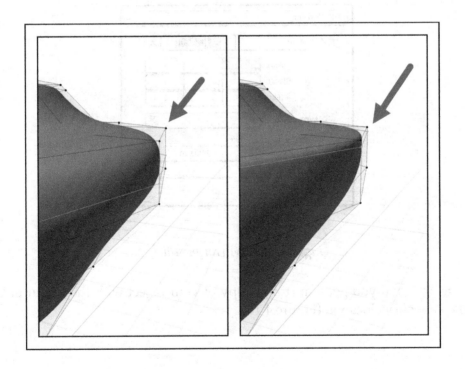

Figure 4.12 - New loops results

You can use the Loop cut to add new edge loops and control every corner's sharpness whenever you have a model that receives a Subdivision Surface Modifier. Having two edge loops close to each other creates a sharper edge.

Tip: You can easily select edge loops in Blender by holding the ALT key while selecting an edge. Blender tries to select all connected edges in a loop.

4.3 Mirror modifier

Another important option from the modifiers list of tools is the Mirror modifier. Unlike the Mirror tool, you can apply using the CTRL+M keys. We get a copy of your selected object using the Mirror modifier, instead of an inverted 3D model.

To use the modifier, select the object you wish to mirror and assign the modification. You must pick an axis from the settings to create the mirror copy (Figure 4.13).

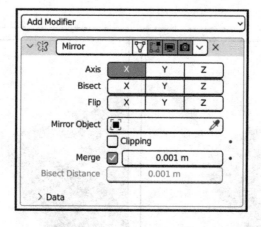

Figure 4.13 - Mirror modifier

Choose the axis, and you get a mirrored copy of your object with the origin point as the pivot for the new object location (Figure 4.14).

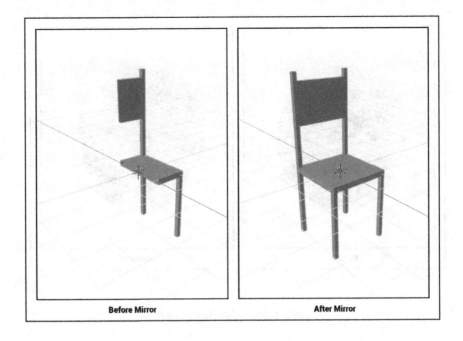

Figure 4.14 - *Mirror results*

The location of your origin point is the main reference to place your mirrored copy. In Figure 4.14, the origin point is at the left side of our object. If the origin point was distant from the object, your copies would also appear at the same distance.

The origin point works as a pivot point. It uses the same base distance from any source object.

After adding a Mirror modifier to any object, you can make that copy and source model a single object using the Apply option. That removes the modifier from the list and joins both objects. Look to the Merge Limit option in the Mirror settings to set a minimum distance to merge vertices from the two sides.

4.3.1 Modifiers order in the stack

Sometimes, your workflow requires other modifiers to create a more complex 3D model. The order in which you add a modifier could impact the final result. For instance, in Figure 4.15, you can see an object receiving a *Mirror* first and then a *Subdivision Surface*.

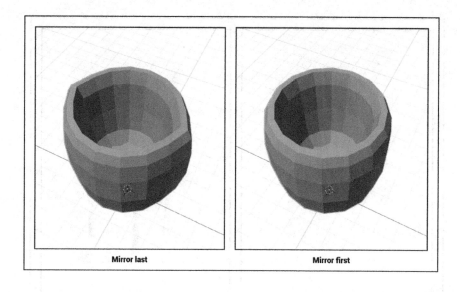

Mirror last   Mirror first

Figure 4.15 - *Modifiers order*

Notice how the model with a *Mirror* as the first modifier displays a much better 3D topology showing a regular and smooth shape.

It will first generate a mirrored copy and then a smoothed surface. Always consider the order in which you will use modifiers to change the surface of an object. In any case, you can change the order of the modifiers by clicking and dragging each modifier from the list. Use the tiny dots on the top right corner of each modifier.

4.4 Array modifier

If you have a shape formed by smaller objects organized in a matrix style, you can use an Array modifier to create such a model. With the Array, we can get any object copied in multiple axes. For instance, if we use the form shown in Figure 4.16 and apply an Array Modifier. You get several copies of that shape repeated side by side.

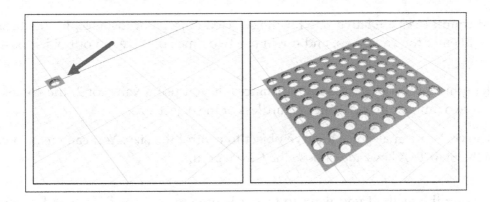

Figure 4.16 - *Shape with Array*

Select the object first and add the modifier to use an Array for modeling. Once the Array modifier is assigned, change the settings to make copies of the object (Figure 4.17).

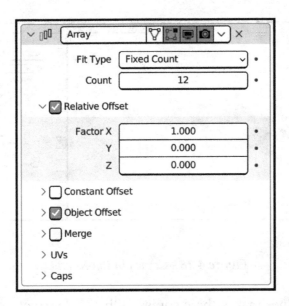

Figure 4.17 - *Array options*

At the top, you have the count that controls the number of copies. There are three main types of methods available for duplicating models:

- **Fixed count**: Uses a relative size for the selected object. For instance, in the distance, you will enter the value two, and it will use two times the size of your object as a distance.

- **Fit length**: Here, you get absolute distances. If you use a value of 2, the copies will stay at two units from each other regardless of the object size.

- **Fit Curve**: You can also use a curve object to control the size. You can create a curve with the SHIFT+A keys and choose the Curve group.

After choosing the method you want to use, it is time to pick the values and axis used to place each duplicate. For instance, in the *Factor X* field, you can set the value used for copies in the X-axis. If you use a value of 1 for the X and 3 for the count, you will get five copies on the X-axis.

Using the Fixed Count type, they will repeat three times on the X-axis (Figure 4.18).

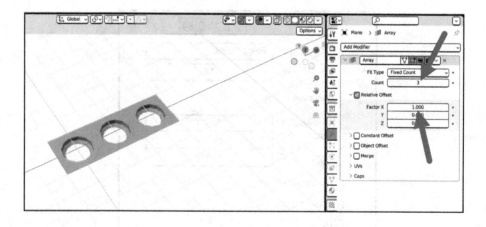

Figure 4.18 - Copies in the X-axis

Using those same values makes three copies with a distance of one unit in the X-axis if you choose Fit Length.

A single Array Modifier will only make copies in either a row or column of objects. You need two Arrays to get a bi-dimensional pattern (rows and columns). For instance, we can use one Array for the X-axis and another for the Y-axis (Figure 4.19).

116

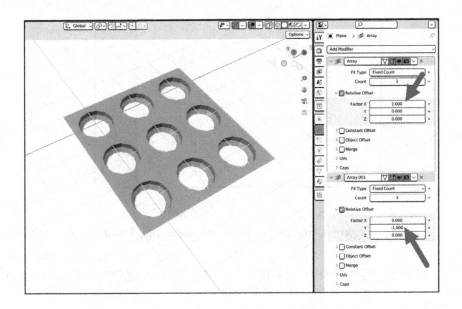

Figure 4.19 - *Copies with two Arrays*

That is the easiest way to get a matrix-style set of copies. If you wish to duplicate the same object in the Z-axis, add another Array Modifier and use the *Factor Z* to set a distance.

4.4.1 Arrays and reference objects

Besides using values to control an Array's distance, you can also use an object to set ranges and rotations for any Array. It could be an existing 3d Model from your scene or a helper object like an Empty from Blender.

An Empty is a unique object in Blender that is invisible in rendering. It works only as a helper for modeling, animation, or any other task requiring a reference object.

You can create an Empty using the SHIFT+A key and choose an Empty with the option *Plain Axis* for the most simple representation (Figure 4.20).

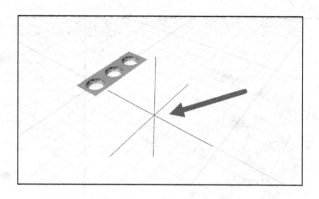

Figure 4.20 - *Empty object to use in the Array*

How can an Empty help us with an Array? At the Array options, you have a field called Object Offset. Use the Empty as the Object Offset.

We can use any object from the scene in Blender as the Object Offset, which controls distance, rotation, and scaling. The Empty is convenient for offering an invisible reference object.

For instance, if you have an existing Array and add an Empty to the Object Offset field, it will immediately control your Array. Rotating and moving the Empty creates a unique shape using the Array (Figure 4.21).

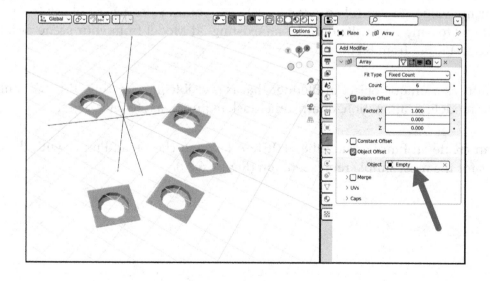

Figure 4.21 - *Array with Empty*

Once you enable the Object Offset in the Array options, use the text field or eyedropper to pick an object by name. Choose the name for the Empty, which will probably be "Empty."

Adding animation data to the Empty can generate interesting abstract animations using the Array. You will learn more about animation with Blender in Chapter 7.

Tip: Remember that you can easily rename any object in your project using the F2 key. Select the object and press the key to assign a new name.

4.5 Boolean modifier

Another useful modifier for 3D modeling is the Boolean, which allows you to create models based on object area interactions. The modifier creates new shapes based on the following:

- Intersections

- Subtractions

- Unions

The 3D objects created from those interactions would be difficult to create using "traditional" modeling techniques. For most operations, you need at least two objects, which you must select by name. As a reminder, you can easily set unique names for 3D models with the F2 key.

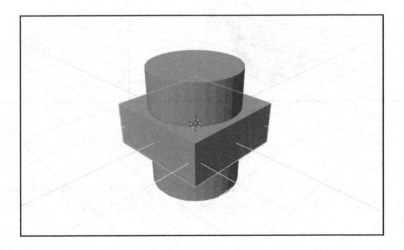

Figure 4.22 - Objects for Boolean

One of the most typical uses of the Boolean Modifier is to open round holes in 3D objects. For that task, you need an object to modify and a cylinder. Place the cylinder at the same location where you want to open the hole (Figure 4.22).

After placing both objects:

1. Assign the Boolean modifier to the object that should receive the hole.

2. Set the Operation as Difference to subtract the shape from another object.

3. Add the cylinder as the second object pointing it by its name at the Object field (Figure 4.23).

At first, you won't notice any changes to either object because the Boolean applies the modification in real-time.

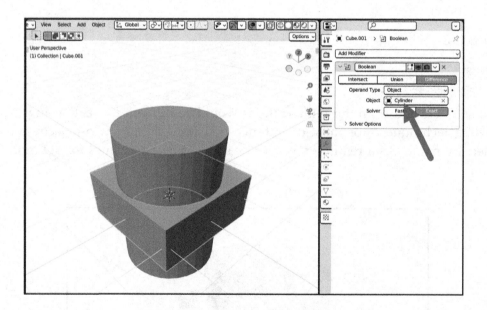

Figure 4.23 - Boolean settings

You must use the Apply option to make the change permanent, and after moving the base object, you will see the hole with the same shape as your cylinder (Figure 4.24).

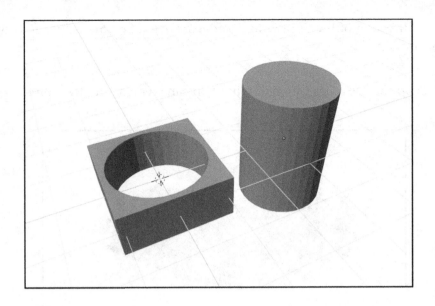

Figure 4.24 - *Boolean results*

The Union option creates a new shape based on the merge of two existing objects, and with the Intersect, you will get a new shape based on the shared space between two 3D models.

4.6 Spin tool for rounded shapes

In cases where you need parts of a model to have a perfectly rounded shape, it will be hard to use only a combination of extrudes and Subdivision Surfaces. In Blender, we have a tool called Spin that can help creating perfectly rounded shapes. The Spin works like an extrude that follows a circular path.

As a result, you get an arch shape for the selected object. Using the Spin is easy if you follow a few rules to create each shape:

– The Spin uses the 3D Cursor as the rotation and arch center pivot point.

– Select the appropriate axis to perform the spin operation. Usually the perpendicular axis based on the rotation of your selection.

– Use the small menu on the lower left of your 3D Viewport to control the segmentation and angle for the Spin.

– Control the direction of the Spin with positive or negative values for the Angle value at the Spin options.

In Figure 4.25, you can see an example of what you can create using the Spin.

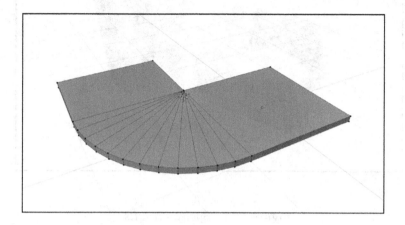

Figure 4.25 - Rounded shape from the Spin

To use the Spin, you must go into Edit Mode and select your model's parts to replicate with the Spin. For instance, we can choose the face of a shape like the one shown in Figure 4.26 (*Left*).

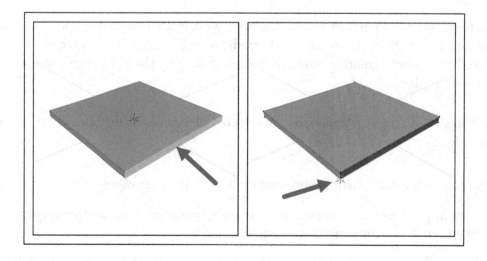

Figure 4.26 - Face for the Spin

Once you have the selected elements, which could also be a set of edges or vertices, you must place the 3D Cursor. Move the 3D Cursor location to the point you wish to use as the pivot in your Spin rotation (Figure 4.26 - *Right*).

The easiest way to move your 3D Cursor to that location is by using the Snap tool (*SHIFT+S*). Before you trigger the Spin from the Toolbar of your 3D Viewport, you must set your view from the object to the top. Press the seven key on your Numpad.

Always consider the plane where your Spin will occur. The view you have must be perpendicular to that plane. In our case, the Spin happens in the X and Y-axis plane. For that reason, using the Top view is the best option. By changing the view, you make your editing process easier.

When in the top view, press the Spin button. A blue arc appears close to the selected elements. Click and drag your mouse above the arch to see your round shape appearing. At the Spin options on the lower-left corner, you can control the rounded shape's rotation and steps (Figure 4.27).

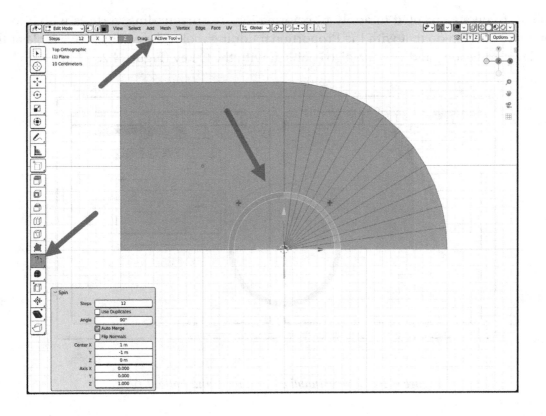

Figure 4.27 - Spin shape results

When you observe a blue arc, it's an indicator that your rotation is anchored to the Z-axis. To toggle between axes, head over to the top left section of your 3D Viewport to change the rotation reference. Switching to the X or Y-axis will correspondingly produce red or green arcs.

Ensure you get all the options and settings for the Spin right after you make the Spin because the menu disappears after you start another operation in Blender. In the Spin menu, you find an option called "Use Duplicates "that doesn't connect the Spin's copies. It works like a rotation-based Array.

4.7 Proportional editing

The transformations we apply to any polygon elements in Blender fully affect selected shapes; they will not influence anything in their surroundings if not selected. For instance, if you choose a couple of vertices from a polygon with hundreds of vertices and press the S key, it will apply a scale only to the selected vertices.

What if you also wanted to apply transformations to surrounding vertices with a lower influence? You can do that with the Proportional Editing tools. The option is available at the 3D Viewport header, and you can also enable it with the O key (Figure 4.28 - *Left*).

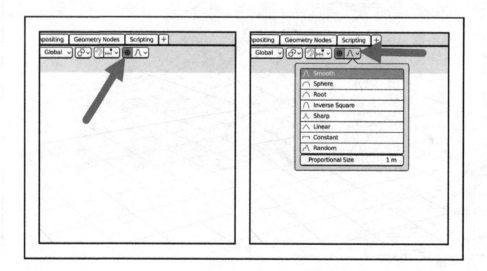

Figure 4.28 - Proportional editing tools and Fallout types

After enabling the Proportional Editing, you must choose a falloff type from the options next to the icon where you trigger the Proportional Editing tools (Figure 4.28 - *Right*).

By enabling Proportional Editing and using as fallout type the smoothing option, you can select a couple of vertices from a plane with multiple subdivisions. Start a move transformation in the Z-axis with the G and Z keys. As a result, the surrounding vertices will also move up (Figure 4.29).

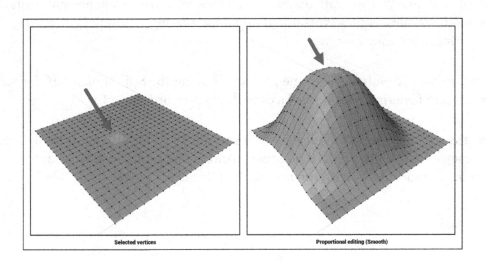

Figure 4.29 - *Proportional editing vertices*

You will notice a small circle around the selected vertex while transforming, showing the area of influence for the Proportional Editing. It is possible to increase or decrease the influence using your mouse wheel or the plus and minus keys from your Numpad.

You can create a plane like the one shown in Figure 4.34 with the Context menu:

1. Select the plane and go to Edit Mode.

2. In Edit Mode, press the A key to select all vertices, and with a right-click, open the Context menu.

3. There, you will choose the first option, called Subdivision.

Each time you choose the Subdivision, you will get the edges of a model divided once. Apply multiple of those Subdivisions to get a high-density mesh.

What is next?

Congratulations on completing Chapter 4! With this, you've reached the midpoint of our guide. You've successfully acquainted yourself with some of Blender's most celebrated tools for 3D modeling. The modifiers discussed in this chapter have opened doors to a myriad of possibilities, enabling you to craft distinctive shapes and three-dimensional artifacts. The beauty of modifiers lies in their versatility - imagine pairing a Subdivision Surface with a Boolean to achieve intricate designs.

Furthermore, you've embarked on the journey of using the Spin tool, adept for sculpting arc structures and fostering organic surfaces with the proportional edit.

Yet, there's an element of authenticity that seems elusive. Our models, although detailed, still feel somewhat synthetic, devoid of a real-world essence. Fear not, as Chapter 5 is dedicated to imbuing our models with life and context through the magic of Materials and Textures.

Chapter 5 - Materials and Textures

Progressing through the initial segments of this guide, you've acquired a solid grasp on Blender's foundational elements and dabbled in 3D modeling. The journey ahead is geared towards visually enriching our creations, bringing them to life.

Chapter 5 invites you into the enthralling domain of materials and textures. Absent these elements, our 3D illustrations present a plain, undistinguished appearance. But, with the judicious use of materials and textures, we breathe life and narrative into them. Visualize the depth when walls or floors are endowed with specific materials.

Our introductory topic is shaders. Here, you'll familiarize yourself with Blender's integral shaders, discerning their unique applications. Transitioning from shaders, we'll pivot to textures, particularly harnessing external images as material finishes.

Digging deeper into the world of textures, you'll become adept at managing these elements using mapping techniques. Subsequently, our path leads to PBR textures, embodying real-world physics for a touch of authenticity. Complement this with nuances like glossy finishes and transparency for an unparalleled sense of realism.

Concluding this chapter, the Asset Browser makes a comeback. Beyond its initial purpose of curating 3D models, learn its utility in safeguarding materials, setting the stage for their future reapplication.

Here's a summary of what you will learn:

- Adding materials to objects and understanding their role.

- Using image textures effectively, including projection and tiling.

- Understanding and using PBR textures in Blender.

- Creating Transparent, Glass, and Glossy surfaces.

- Attaching textures to the Blender file for portability.

- Applying multiple materials for complex surfaces.

- Managing and accessing materials with the Asset Browser.

5.1 Adding materials to objects

Any scene in Blender can benefit from good lighting and realistic materials. With the materials tab, you have plenty of tools and options to assign shaders, textures, and other effects to give visual context for surfaces.

For instance, if you have to create a 3D model that should appear as a stone wall, you can use a texture on that object to make it look like a stone wall. We can create all types of surfaces based on a combination of shaders, effects, and textures.

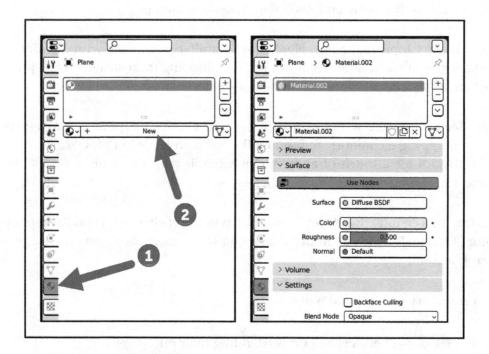

Figure 5.1 - *Material tab and editor*

Before we start to handle material creation and shaders, it is essential to define a few aspects of materials in Blender:

– A material must have one or multiple objects assigned.

– You can remove a material from an object. If a material doesn't have any assigned objects, Blender will purge that material when you save and close the project file.

– Multiple objects can use the same material.

– Each material must receive a unique name to help you visually identify what it represents.

– You can reuse materials in other projects using the Append or Link options from the File menu.

To create a Blender material, select an object first and then go to the Material tab (1) in the Properties Editor (Figure 5.1).

At the Material tab, you will see a button to create a new material (2) or a list with options to edit any existing materials assigned to the selected 3D model (Figure 5.1 - *Right*).

For objects with a material, multiple controls are available to manage the material at the top (Figure 5.2).

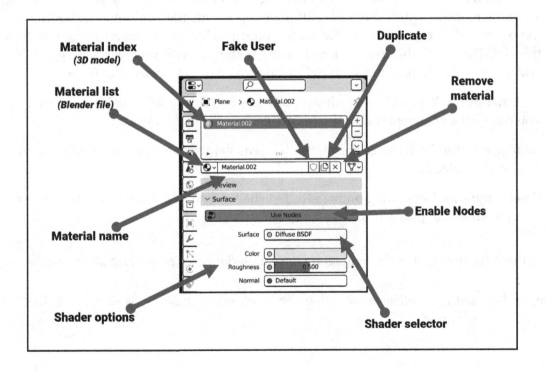

Figure 5.2 - *Material controls*

Here is a list of what you can do with each of the controls:

- **Material Name:** In the text field, you can rename the material. Assigning meaningful names for materials is crucial, which will help you later identify what they represent.

- **Remove:** With this button, you can remove the material from the object. It won't erase the material. If it doesn't have any objects assigned, Blender will purge the material the next time you exit the software.

- **Duplicate:** In some cases, you may want to create a new material using another one as a template. You can create a copy of the existing material with the duplicate button.

- **Fake user:** Any material that doesn't have an object assigned will be at risk of deletion when you close Blender. You can enable the Fake User to keep any material from getting purged, even if it has no objects assigned.

- **Enable Nodes:** Makes all information from a material appear at the Shader Editor using Nodes. Later in this chapter, we will learn how to use Nodes.

- **Material list:** All your materials will become part of the Blender file you are working on at the moment. This button lists all materials in this file, and you can easily reuse them. Instead of creating new materials, you can select an object and pick one from this list. The list is also helpful for showing materials with no objects assigned. You will see a zero right next to a material that doesn't have any objects assigned.

- **Material index:** We can have multiple materials in a single object using indexes. Here you have a list of all materials assigned for each index in the object.

- **Shader selector:** Each material can use different shaders, and you can select one from a list in this selector.

- **Shader options:** Depending on the selected shader, you might see different options to set up their visual properties.

Using these controls makes the management of materials a lot easier and allows reuse.

Info: Many materials options work with the same settings regardless of your renderer. That is the case for Cycles and Eevee.

5.2 Materials and Shaders

After you create a material, the first thing you have to do is choose a proper shader. A shader is one of the most critical elements of any material because it controls how the object interacts with light. For instance, you can have a material that behaves like glass or an opaque surface.

What sets the look of any material is the shader you choose from a list of available options (Figure 5.3). Look for the Surface option in the Material tab.

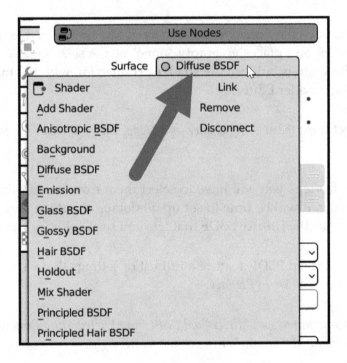

Figure 5.3 - Shader list for Blender

From the list, you will find some shaders like:

– **Diffuse BSDF**: A simple shader that will create an opaque surface absorbing all light.

– **Glossy BSDF**: The shader you will want to use for surfaces with any reflection level, like mirrors and some types of metals.

- **Glass BSDF**: If you need realistic transparency, you will use the Glass BSDF for advanced reflections and light distortion.

- **Emission**: A material that will behave like a light source and contribute to a scene's lighting.

- **Mix Shader**: This option allows you to blend multiple shaders to create unique effects.

- **Transparent BSDF**: If you need simple transparency in materials, you will use the Transparent BSDF.

- **Principled BSDF**: A powerful shader that can create most of the effects alone and be the base for all surfaces using physically-based materials.

On the top right, you have the *Remove* and *Disconnect*. The first option excludes information from the current shader and places an empty "none" as the selection. With the Disconnect, you keep most of the settings but lose the shader's connection with the material. It will still be available from your Shader Editor.

Info: *The disconnect keeps the existing shader as a Node, which you can use from the Shader Editor.*

To use any of the shaders, you will have to select them from the list shown in Figure 5.3. Once you pick a shader, it will be time to set up all details about the surface. Some shaders offer simple controls like the Diffuse BSDF that lets you set a color for the material.

Others, like the Principled BSDF, feature a full list of settings that we will discuss in more detail in section *5.4 PBR texture in Blender*.

Info: *The BSDF acronym means Bidirectional Scattering Distribution Function, which identifies the mathematical function that controls how a surface scatter light.*

5.2.1 Diffuse BSDF (Simple colors)

If you must create materials with only a simple color, add the Diffuse BSDF as a shader. That shader has a color picker; you can get the color you want and use it for any selected 3D object (Figure 5.4).

Notice how each field in the material options has a colored circle on the left side. Those circles and colors identify the type of data you can use for each field. A green circle means a shader and a yellow one means color. The grey and blue represent numeric values and height information, respectively.

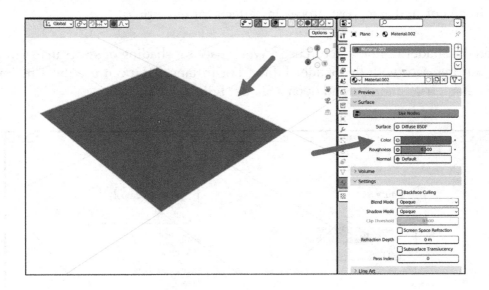

Figure 5.4 - Diffuse BSDF material

Regarding material previews, you can view how the material looks in two locations:

1. At the Material tab, you will see a Preview field displaying the materials in a geometrical primitive.
2. You can also use the 3D Viewport by choosing the Rendered or Material Preview shading mode. Press the Z key and choose Rendered. For real-time previews, make sure you are using Eevee for rendering. That is the default renderer for Blender. You can use Eevee for fast material previews even if you swap for Cycles later.

The Material tab shows all the important options in a vertical list of settings. However, you can also use the Shader Editor for much better flexibility in material creation.

5.2.2 The Shader Editor

The Material tab gives us many options to craft and design materials for any 3D object, but when it is time to create complex surfaces and mix multiple options, we need something more advanced. One of the only ways to get that flexibility is with the Shader Editor.

That is a special type of Editor in Blender that displays data in a workflow style using Nodes for Shaders and material related options. A Node is a small box that collects information about a function, effect, shader, etc. With the Shader Editor, you can edit materials, your environment, and even post-processing effects for rendering.

To open the Shader Editor, you can use a Workspace for shading or swap an existing division in your interface with the Shader Editor. For instance, you can use the Timeline area from the default user interface and open a Shader Editor (Figure 5.5).

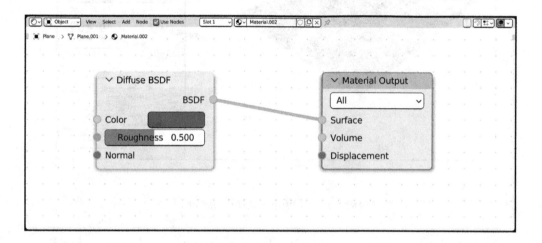

Figure 5.5 - *Shader Editor*

With the Shader Editor, you will see blocks of information for materials that receive the name of Node. You connect Nodes like a workflow of information from left to right. For materials, you always have the last Node on a chain as the "Material Output," what comes before this Node will depend on the material you create.

Here are a few crucial facts about Nodes:

– Each Node could have input and output sockets represented by circles on the sides of each Node. For instance, you will see Shaders having both input and output. The "Material Output" Node only has input sockets on the left side.

– The sockets have color codes that identify the data type they can handle. The colors are the same ones from the Material tab.

– You can connect Nodes by clicking and dragging from an output socket to an input. For optimal results, always try to connect sockets from the same color code.

134

- To select and manipulate Nodes, use the same shortcuts from the 3D Viewport.

- You can hold the CTRL key while clicking and dragging with the right mouse button to break a connection. The cursor will turn to a knife, and you can cut links between Nodes.

- You can erase a Node with either the X key or DEL.

- To create new Nodes, use the SHIFT+A key or the Add menu in the Shader Editor.

A simple example of what we can do with the Shader Editor is with the Mix Shader, allowing us to blend two different shaders for a single material. We can mix a Diffuse BSDF and a Glossy BSDF:

1. Select an object and add a new material.

2. Choose the Diffuse BSDF as the Shader.

3. Open the Shader Editor

4. Press the SHIFT+A keys, and from the Shaders group, add a Mix Shader

5. Press the SHIFT+A again, and from the Shaders group, add a Glossy BSDF

You will get the Nodes shown in Figure 5.6 *(Left)*.

We must rearrange the Nodes to connect the Diffuse BSDF and Glossy BSDF to the Mix Shader. The Mix Shader connects to the Material Output.

To connect Nodes, we have two options:

- You can break the connection from the Diffuse BSDF to the Material Output by holding the CTRL key while clicking and dragging with the right mouse button. Click and drag from the Diffuse and Glossy output sockets to the Mix Shader. Connect the Mix Shader to the Material Output.

- Since the Diffuse BSDF already has a connection to the Material Output, move the Mix Shader Node until it is above the connection line between the Diffuse BSDF and Material Output. You will see the line becoming highlighted, and if you release the Mix Shader, it rearranges the connections and stay between both Nodes. You can connect the Glossy BSDF to the Mix Shader once the Diffuse has a connection.

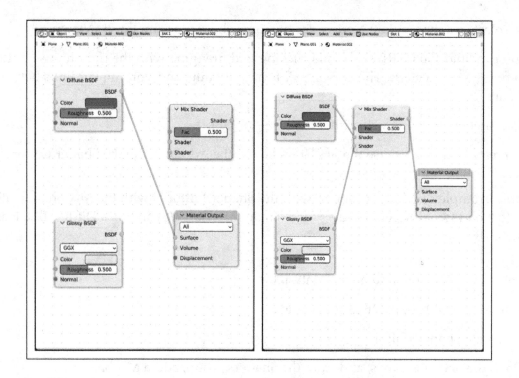

Figure 5.6 - *Nodes with no connections*

Both options produce the same result, as shown in Figure 5.6 *(Right)*. The handling of all other Nodes and materials uses similar settings and procedures. By the way, you can do the same thing with the Material tab. From the Shaders settings, you can choose the Mix Shader (Figure 5.7).

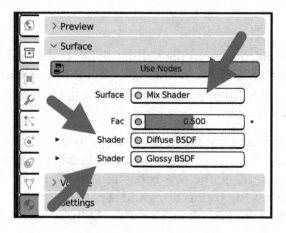

Figure 5.7 - *Mix Shader in the Material Editor*

You can select the two Shaders composing a material in the Mix Shader. You have the option to use either the Material tab or Shader Editor. The advantage of using the Shader Editor is that it works more visually and gives you an edge when using complex materials with multiple Nodes.

Adding another Mix Shader to any slots allows you to blend even more Nodes in a material. The same applies to the Shader Editor, where you can add more Mix Shader Nodes or duplicate an existing Node with the SHIFT+D keys to compose more complex materials.

5.3 Using image textures

Using the Shaders alone won't produce realistic results for some surfaces, where an image texture is the best choice. To add an image texture to any material, use a Node called "Image Texture."

Info: *From this point forward, we will use mainly the Shader Editor to craft materials. But you will get the same results with the Material tab.*

To add an Image Texture Node to the material, press the SHIFT+A key or use the Add menu in the Shader Editor. Go to the Texture group and choose Image Texture (Figure 5.8).

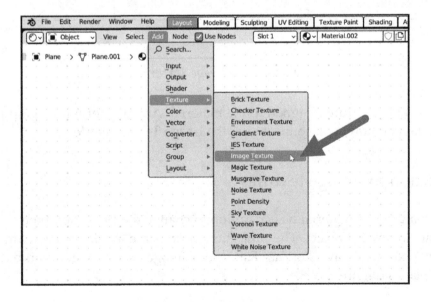

Figure 5.8 - *Image Texture Node*

You will click the "Open" button (1) to pick an image file from your hard drive or a local network from the Node. After opening a texture file, connect the Texture Node to the input socket (2) of your Diffuse BSDF (Figure 5.9).

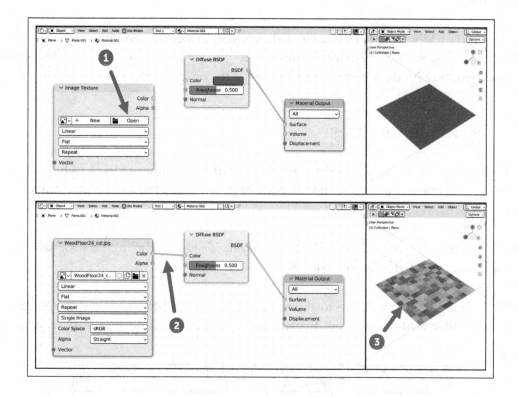

Figure 5.9 - *Image Texture*

The result will be a texture assigned to the material. Any Shader with an input socket receiving color data (Yellow) will connect with the Image Texture Node.

5.3.1 Projection for image textures

Each image you use in a material has an option to change the projection type, which affects how it appears in any 3D object. The projection options are available at the Image Texture Node and, by default, always start as "Flat." Your image will look good on bidimensional surfaces like planes (Figure 5.10).

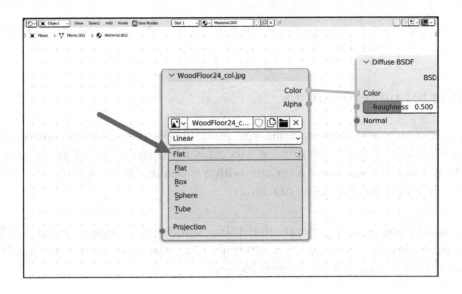

Figure 5.10 - *Projection options*

However, using "Flat" in shapes that also have a depth might result in distortions. You can choose other types of projections that match multiple objects' shape. A common choice for 3D models with textures is the "Box," which will consider an object as a whole (Figure 5.11).

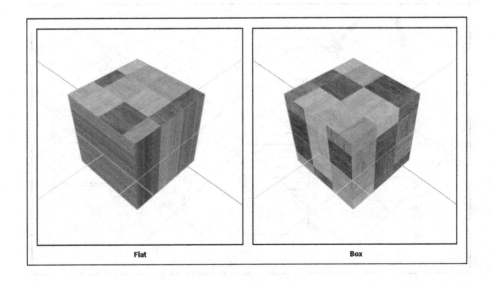

Figure 5.11 - *Box projection*

You can use the other two mapping options for the cases with a spherical or cylindrical 3D model; Sphere or Cylinder.

5.3.2 Tilling for image textures

After assigning a texture to any material, you probably want additional controls for certain visual aspects of that image. One of those aspects is the distribution of an image at any 3D model surface. Usually, you want a texture with a repeating pattern that can cover a large surface. The technique has the name of tilling.

Unless you add controls to generate that tilling effect, image-based textures will not re-peat on a surface. Instead, all images stretch to fit all available areas of a surface. To create a tilling effect, you will need two additional Nodes:

– From the Input → **Texture Coordinates**

– From the Vector → **Mapping**

Connect the Generated output socket from the Texture Coordinates to the Mapping. From the Mapping, you will connect it to the Image Texture (Figure 5.12).

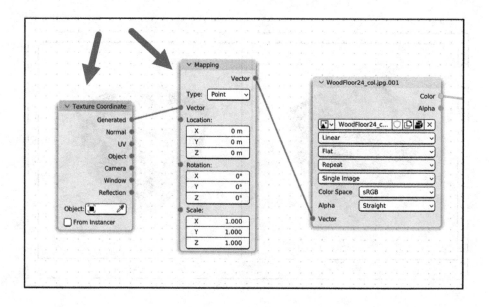

Figure 5.12 - Tilling controls Nodes

To control the tilling of textures, we use the Scale field from the Mapping Node. If you increase the size for the scale, the Mapping multiplies the textures in the same region; for instance, by using a scale of two for all axis in a Cube, resulting in two textures side by side on all axis (Figure 5.13).

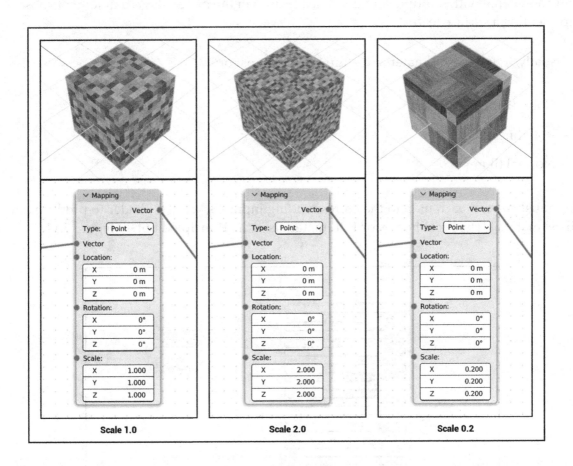

Figure 5.13 - Texture tilling controls with the Scale

If you want to increase your textures' size, use smaller values like "0.5," which will cut in half the size of your textures.

Tip: To use textures with tilling, you should always look for seamless texture images. Those textures won't show visible borders when placed side by side.

5.4 PBR textures in Blender

You must use a particular type of material for projects requiring maximum surface realism. This material has the name PBR, and the acronym means "Physically Based Render," identifying a material with multiple textures. Each texture in the material has a unique purpose of representing a surface feature.

Usually, a simple PBR material feature texture maps for:

– Color (Diffuse)

– Roughness

– Normal (Bump)

You must connect each map to the corresponding input socket of a Shader to produce a realistic material. The best Shader for PBR materials is the Principled BSDF (Figure 5.14).

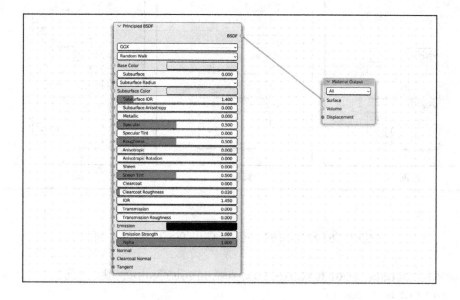

Figure 5.14 - Principled BSDF

Before we start using PBR materials, you must find some of those special textures. A PBR material usually comes with multiple of those maps available. Several online libraries offer free PBR materials. Some of the best sources for PBR materials:

- ambientcg.com

- polyhaven.com/textures

- cgbookcase.com

They provide high-quality PBR textures in the public domain with resolutions going up to 8k (8.192 pixels):

- **1K**: 1024 x 1024 pixels

- **2K**: 2048 x 2048 pixels

- **4K**: 4096 x 4096 pixels

- **8K**: 8192 x 8192 pixels

PBR textures are characterized by their uniform square proportions across all related images. This uniformity eases the task of tiling these images, with most being seamlessly designed, ensuring they fit together without obvious junctions.

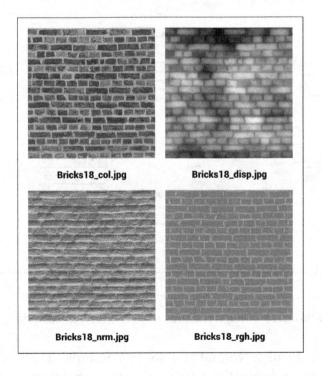

Figure 5.15 - *PBR material files example*

On downloading these textures, expect to receive them bundled in a zip format. To make these images accessible, extract the compressed file to your local storage. Post extraction, you'll notice each image tagged with a suffix, helping identify its map type (Figure 5.15).

The naming pattern for each texture map may change based on your textures' source, but they will most likely follow the same types of names.

To set up a PBR surface, create a new material, and choose the Principled BSDF as the shader. Add an Image Texture Node by pressing the SHIFT+A key in the Shader Editor. You can also drag and drop the image file from your file manager to the Shader Editor.

Dragging image files to the Shader Editor makes Blender automatically create an Image Texture Node with that image as the source.

Select the first Texture Node and press SHIFT+D twice for the remaining Image Texture Nodes. It creates two copies of the Image Texture Node. Or drag and drop the remaining image textures to the Shader Editor (Figure 5.16).

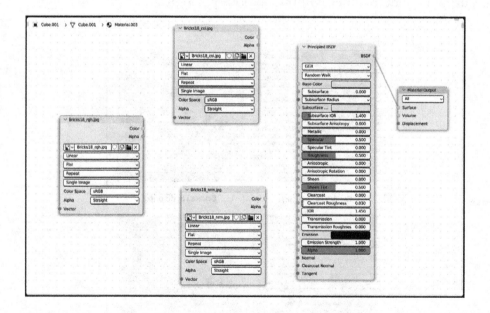

Figure 5.16 - *Image Textures in the PBR material settings*

We use a PBR material with a Normal map for this example. The Normal and Roughness maps don't affect colors, so change the color space settings to "Non-Color" (Figure 5.17).

144

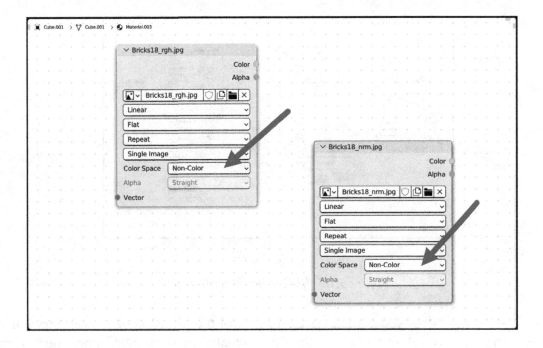

Figure 5.17 - Color Settings for the Normal and Roughness

After setting the Color Space, we can start connecting the Image Texture Nodes to the Principled BSDF:

1. Connect the Color textures to the Base Color

2. Connect the Roughness texture to the Roughness

We need an additional Node for the Normal Texture, which you can create from the Vector group. Press SHIFT+A and add a Normal Map Node:

1. Connect the Normal texture to the Normal Map

2. Connect the Normal Map to the Normal

At the end of the process, you should have a Node setup like Figure 5.18 shows.

145

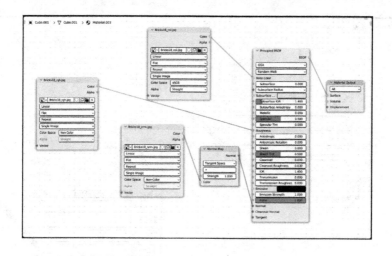

Figure 5.18 - PBR material with maps

With the Normal Map Node, it is possible to control the direction of your Bump. For instance, using negative values will invert the ridges created by the map. Change the Strength value to control the height of a normal map.

5.4.1 Adding tilling and mapping controls

With the Texture Coordinates and Mapping, you can add tilling control to the PBR material. Connect the Mapping to each one of the Image Textures for full control (Figure 5.19).

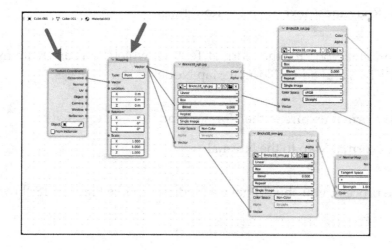

Figure 5.19 - Tilling control

As part of the control process for tilling textures, you have to keep connecting the Mapping Node to any new Image Texture Node. If you miss a connecting to the Mapping to an Image Texture, it can generate odd visuals on the material.

5.4.2 Ambient occlusion maps

You will also find additional maps like AO (Ambient Occlusion) in some PBR textures. Depending on the type and source of your texture, you might find those extra maps. Those images connect with specific input sockets for the Principled BSDF.

The Ambient Occlusion connects to the Base Color, where you must use a MixRGB Node from the Color group to blend it with the color map (Figure 5.20). For the MixRGB, use the Multiply option.

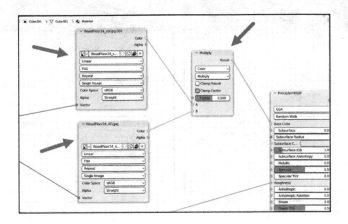

Figure 5.20 - *Ambient Occlusion map*

Most of the PBR materials offer the same types of maps regarding textures. It is a matter of following the same pattern with Image Texture Nodes and a Principled BSDF. You will be able to create dozens of PBR materials easily. It is possible to design a template in a material with all Nodes ready, but no actual texture files selected, to save time during this process.

Duplicate that "blank" material and assign all texture files to start a new PBR setup. Whenever you have to assemble a new material, it can save a few minutes.

Tip: It is also possible to "import" materials from other files in Blender. Use the File → Append or File → Link options to incorporate or reference existing materials. Select a Blender file and navigate to the "Materials" folder. Select the materials you wish to use and reuse them in new projects.

5.5 Transparent and glass materials

For materials that require transparency, you can use options like the Glass BSDF and Transparency BSDF. With the Transparency BSDF, you will get materials with a simple effect that doesn't divert light (Figure 5.21 - *Left*).

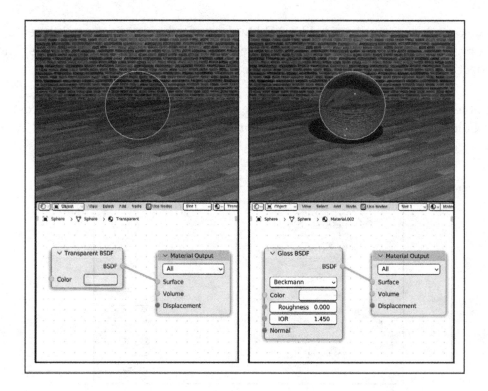

Figure 5.21 - Transparent and Glass BSDF (Cycles)

If you need more sophisticated transparency, you should pick the Glass BSDF. The shader has two settings that will help you achieve a more realistic effect:

- **IOR**: An index that controls the refraction of light.
- **Roughness**: Here, you can control the smoothness of your surface reflection. Values close to zero will create a polished glass surface, and higher values will make it look grainy.

A material with Glass BSDF can produce realistic results with advanced transparency (Figure 5.21 - *Right*). Use the IOR settings to control how the light diverts from your model's interior using a material with a Glass BSDF. You can also mix shaders to achieve unique effects using transparency.

5.6 Glossy surfaces

If you want a surface with a certain level of reflection, you must use either a Glossy BSDF or the Principled BSDF. Both shaders feature settings that control how your material will reflect light: *roughness*.

A material with a roughness close to zero has a perfect reflection, almost like a mirror. For higher values, it starts to get a blurred reflection until you can't identify the objects reflected anymore (Figure 5.22).

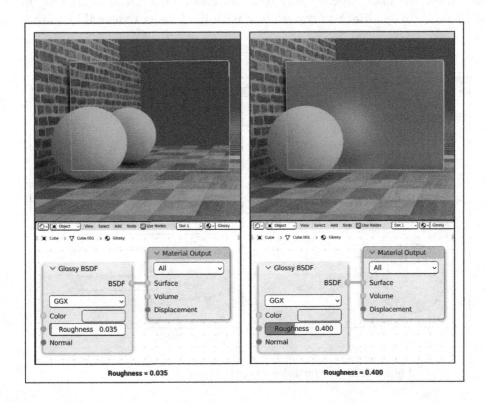

Figure 5.22 - *Comparing the roughness values in the Glossy BSDF*

If you want a perfect mirror in a material, set the Roughness to zero and the color from the Glossy BSDF color to black.

5.7 Attaching textures to the Blender file

Any image-based texture added to materials in Blender is an external resource for your main project file. It is possible to manage and handle those files independently from Blender. If you back up the Blender project file alone, it won't have any image texture files used for materials unless you merge them into a single file.

For instance, if you want to copy Blender project files to an external hard drive or send them to a cloud storage service, all texture files must follow the Blender file to the same location. Usually, it is a good practice to place those files in the same folder. That way, you can back up and copy the entire folder simultaneously.

It makes handling external data easier for large projects, especially if you must move the project file somewhere else. An easy way to avoid all that trouble is to attach your external files to the Blender project file. You can do that with the **File → External Data** menu (Figure 5.23 - *Left*).

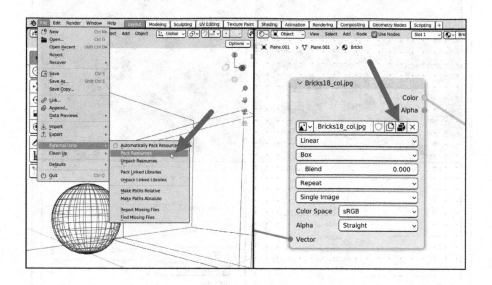

Figure 5.23 - External data options and Nodes with icon

An option called "Pack All Into .blend" attaches all external resources to the Blender project file, making both Blender files and image textures a single file. They will work as if they were a ZIP that has multiple files inside.

Info: An external file with a path starting with "//"has a relative path and will most likely come from the same folder of your project file.

After using that option, you won't have to worry about external files anymore because all textures are part of your project file. However, it may significantly increase the size of your project file. If you have a project file with 1MB in size and 300MB of textures, the new project file size will be 301 MB.

To automate the packing of external data, you can enable the "Automatically Pack All Into .blend." Use the "Unpack All Into Files" to extract the files to your project folder.

There is also an option to unpack texture files next to the image filename individually. At the Image Texture Node, you will see a button called Unpack Item (Figure 5.23 - *Right*). Press this icon to extract one image file to the project folder.

Tip: When Blender can't find a texture file, it will show a pink color at your texture location. The visual code represents an error where a file is missing. You will have to replace the texture to fix that pink color, which could appear in materials or any other location where you can insert texture files.

5.8 Using multiple materials

What if you want to apply multiple materials to a single object? When you have an object that must receive multiple materials, it is time to use material indexes at the top of your Material tab. We can use a simple model like the one shown in Figure 5.24 to show how to use multiple materials with the same object.

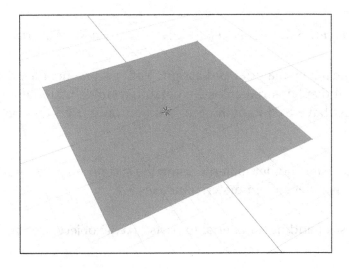

Figure 5.24 - *Model with multiple faces*

How to create an object like this one? Add a **Mesh → Plane** to the scene using the SHIFT+A keys. In Edit Mode, select all vertices, and, with a right-click, open the Context menu. Choose the Subdivide option a few times to create multiple divisions.

You will see additional options in the Material tab when you select any object and go to Edit Mode. Right below your indexes selector, you will see buttons for Assign, Select, and Deselect (Figure 5.25 - *Left*).

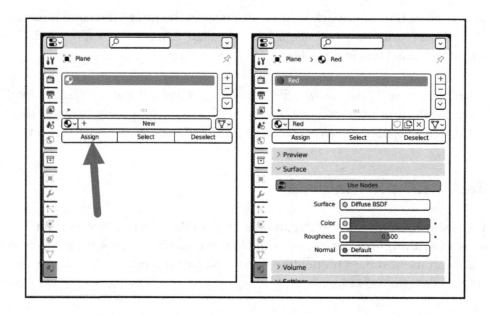

Figure 5.25 - Material tab in Edit Mode and Red Material

For instance, create a new material and assign "Red" as a name. Pick the Diffuse BSDF as a shader and make it display a red color. By default, a single material applies to the entire object, and you don't have to do anything else if you only need that one material (Figure 5.25 - *Right*).

However, we can create another material using the second material index for this selected object. Each object has independent material indexes.

To start the process of adding a material to parts of a 3D object, we can follow these steps referring to Figure 5.26:

1. Select the parts you wish apply the material. In our case, select half of the plane.

2. Add another index for that object using the "+" button on the right.

3. Press the Assign button to connect the new index to the selected faces of your 3D model.

4. Select an existing material or create a new one from scratch. We can create a simple " Green " material with a Diffuse BSDF shader and set a green color.

By following these steps, we can use multiple materials in a single 3D model. The key in the process is to connect each index to the selected parts of any object using the Assign button.

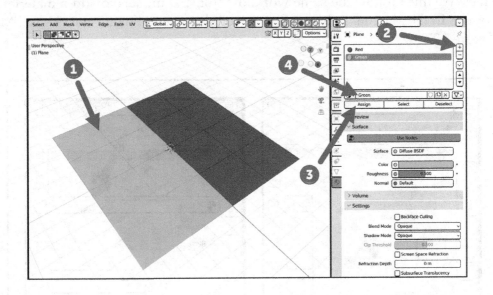

Figure 5.26 - *Green material in half of the 3D model*

By the end of the process, you have an object using two materials. If you need more materials for the object, add new indexes and select other parts of the model. Mark the elements you want to use and press the Assign button.

5.9 Materials in the Asset Browser

In Chapter 2, we introduced the Asset Browser to reuse 3D models using a library. That is one of the best ways to bring data from external Blender files and use it again in new projects. As you probably noticed from all the setup required to create PBR materials, developing and preparing each unique texture involves a lot of time.

By using the Append or Link options, we can quickly bring those materials from other Blender files, but with no visual reference, and you would need to remember the following:

- Location of each Blender file

- If that Blender file has the material you need

- The textures used for that material

The Asset Browser is the easiest and most reliable way to bring materials from external Blender files. We must follow the same workflow from 3D models to add a material to the Asset Browser. In the Material Editor, right-click on the material name and choose "Mark as Asset" (Figure 5.27).

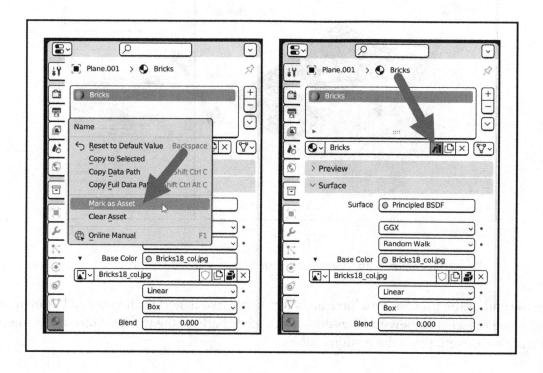

Figure 5.27 - Marking materials as Assets

A library icon next to the material name appears, which means it is ready for the Asset Browser. From this point forward, you can save the Blender file in a folder that is part of a library. You can create separate libraries for materials in the **Edit → Preferences** menu. Go to the *File Paths* tab and add the folder as a library for materials.

If you open the Asset Browser now, you will see your materials listed as part of the Library (Figure 5.28).

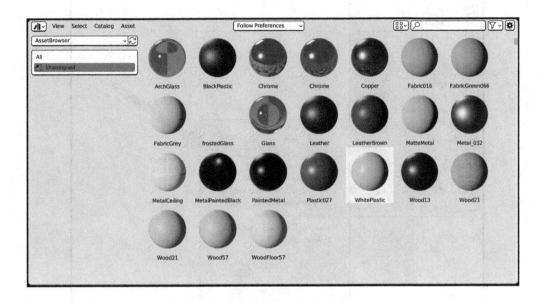

Figure 5.28 - *Materials in the Asset Browser*

How to apply materials from the Asset Browser to objects in Blender? You can click and drag the material in the object. This action even supports objects with multiple channels. For instance, you can click and drag a material to a part of an object with a separate channel. That way, you only have the material applied to a part of that object.

5.10 Using USDZ files with packed PBR textures

As you probably noticed from adding and setting up PBR materials in Blender, it takes a lot of work and time to import and set up all the Nodes required to create a surface. If you want to keep adding PBR textures and need a faster way to make those materials, in a recent update to Blender, we got support for USDZ files. If you look into **Blender's File** → **Import** options, you find a section with USD files (Figure 5.29).

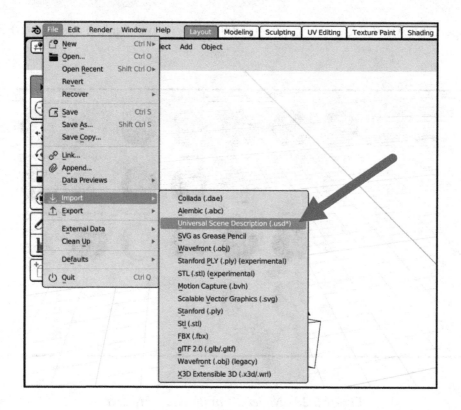

Figure 5.29 - *Importing USD files*

What is this type of file? The USD acronym means *Universal Scene Description*, a format created by Pixar. There are lots of variations for that file:

– USD

– USDA

– USDZ

In the context of PBR textures, you should closely examine the USDZ variant. What is so special about the USDZ file? It works as a compressed version of a scene file, which can include multiple assets like textures and external resources.

Since the format is relatively new, you won't find many locations offering USDZ files for download. However, we can use the entire library from ambientcg.com as USDZ files since the author of that site saved all of the assets using the same format.

For instance, we can pick any asset like this one:

– https://ambientcg.com/view?id=WoodFloor051

We have to set up a wood floor texture with many different texture maps individually in Blender to create a PBR material using those maps. If you try downloading any version of this texture, you will find all variations as ZIP files. The trick is to rename the ZIP to USDZ.

After renaming the ZIP file, you can go to the **File → Import → Universal Scene Description** in Blender and find that same file. After selecting the texture file (1), you must enable the "Import All Materials" option in the import dialog (2) (Figure 5.30).

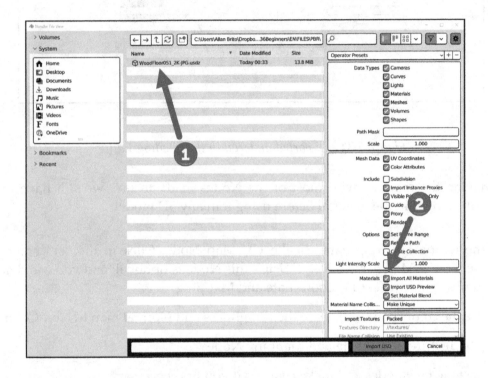

Figure 5.30 - Enable the import options in the USDZ

If you don't enable this option, you won't be able to see the material in the Materials Editor.

Once you import the USDZ file, open the Material Editor, and you should probably see a new material there with the same name used in the downloaded file. To view the details of your material, open the Shader Editor to view the structure of the material (Figure 5.31).

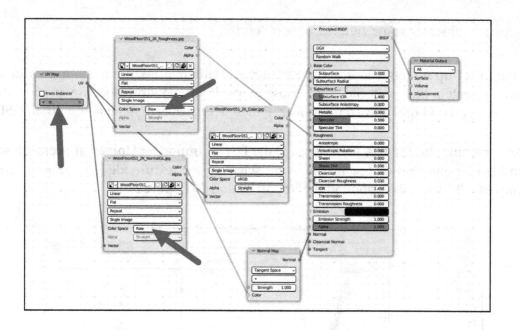

Figure 5.31 - *Imported material in the Shading Editor*

Even having the material with most of the Nodes ready to use, we still have to make some minor changes in the material before using it in any 3D model:

1. Fix the wrong UV Map name in the UV Map Node. Click in the "st" name and choose the UV Map name instead. Using this Node is optional, and you can delete it if you plan to use a Texture Coordinate and Mapping.

2. Update the color space settings in the Roughness and Normal map to Non-Color.

3. Add the Texture Coordinate and Mapping Nodes

4. Connect the new nodes and make changes if you find necessary

Those are simple changes required in the material, but the USDZ format saved us from most of the hard work regarding material setup.

What is next?

For those venturing into the realm of realistic 3D artwork, the integration of materials and textures is paramount. Without them, achieving a life-like render is almost an impossibility. By concluding Chapter 5, you've armed yourself with crucial insights into Blender's materials ecosystem.

You're now equipped with the skills to both craft and manage materials using the dedicated editor. Additionally, tools like the Asset Browser empower you to efficiently reuse and organize your materials. One cannot overlook the impressive adaptability of PBR materials. They might demand an initial time investment, but the outcomes are undeniably outstanding.

As we progress, Chapter 6 delves into rendering within Blender, spotlighting both Cycles and Eevee. Pairing these with meticulously designed materials significantly elevates the potential of your final renders.

Chapter 6 - Rendering and illumination

Rendering and illuminating a scene can be a daunting task for many artists working in Blender. And to add another layer of complexity, you're faced with a choice between two rendering engines: Eevee and Cycles.

In this chapter, we'll navigate the intricacies of deciding between Cycles and Eevee, and set the stage with apt lighting for rendering. To assist you in making an informed decision, we'll demystify the complete process of scene setup using both engines.

Additionally, delve deeper into shading nuances and the art of camera configuration.

Here is a list of what you will learn:

– Differences between Eevee and Cycles

– How to choose Eevee or Cycles for rendering

– Use shading modes and lights for render

– Adjust the focal length from cameras

– Saving renders as images

– Using environment maps

6.1 Rendering and shading modes

Once you have a 3D model with materials and textures, the next step is to get a render. To render a Blender project, you must decide which is the engine you will want to use. The two options available in Blender are:

- Eevee (*default*)

- Cycles

They are both great renderers that can be useful in specific types of projects. You use Cycles for projects that demand light accuracy and cutting-edge realism. All this quality from Cycles has a high cost in terms of computational power.

As a result, we get longer render times with Cycles, ranging from a couple of minutes, hours, or days for single render. The time required to render a scene depends on several factors like your scene's complexity and the hardware used to render.

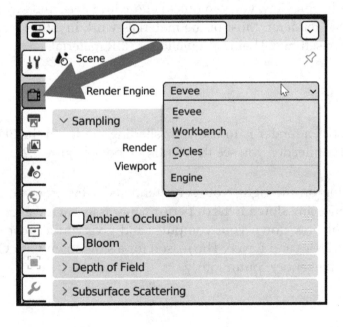

Figure 6.1 - *Render engine selector*

Eevee is the new default renderer, which debuted with Blender 2.8 and can work with real-time visualization. Eevee's technology is closer to what we find in modern 3D games, where you will see a less realistic solution for lights and materials but with incredible speed.

You can choose between Eevee and Cycles at the Render tab in your Properties Editor (Figure 6.1).

By default, you will always start with Eevee as the main render engine, but you can change to Cycles.

Should you choose Eevee or Cycles for rendering? That depends on your main objective for a project. Here is a quick summary between them:

– **Cycles**: Easier to set up and get realistic results, but might require several minutes or hours to get a finished image.
– **Eevee**: Deliver results in real-time but will not get the same level of realism from Cycles, and requires some pre-processing work to display good looking images.

For materials and lights preview, you can quickly go with Eevee and swap later to Cycles if you decide to use that renderer. Most of the materials work in either renderer without the need to change a lot of settings. That is also valid for PBR materials.

6.1.1 Shading modes

The easiest way to start a render is to use your shading modes in the 3D Viewport. If you look to the right of your header, you see the shading modes (Figure 6.2).

With the last button on the right, you get a rendered view from your scene. By using Eevee, you won't notice any slowdowns or performance issues. However, changing the renderer to Cycles might slow down your computer and give you a great impression on the differences between Cycles and Eevee. The reason for a slowdown with Cycles is because it will keep processing the render continuously.

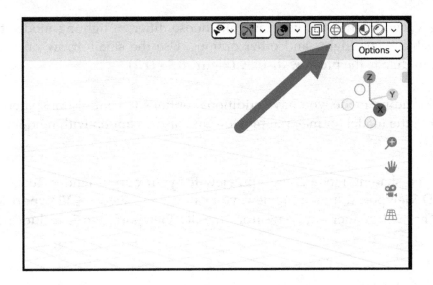

Figure 6.2 - Shading modes

That might get your CPU (*processor*) or GPU (*graphics-card*) usage to 100% load and compromise your computer's performance.

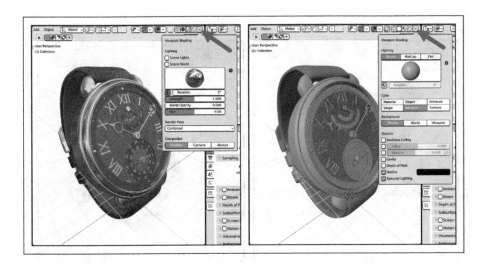

Figure 6.3 - Material Preview options

Suppose you want to have a view if your scene with textures and a rough preview of lights, you can use the Material Preview mode. The shortcut to quickly change shading modes is the Z key.

Regarding Viewport shading, you can still choose different lighting modes for the preview and enable Scene Lights and other options. Use the small arrow on your shading modes' right to change the preview display (Figure 6.3 - *Left*).

With Solid shading mode, you have additional options to control transparency and also use colors from the model for material preview and also an option with random colors (Figure 6.3 - *Right*).

The Rendered shading mode gives a preview for your output render. To save an image from your 3D Viewport during a preview, you can use the **View → Viewport Render Image** menu. That will render any view from the 3D Viewport, and it includes all shading modes.

6.2 Working with cameras

Before we start rendering images from a Blender scene, it is imperative to learn how to manage and adjust cameras. The reason for this is because Blender only renders what the active camera is seeing. That is why you might adjust the view, and when pressing F12 for render, a different angle appears in the render.

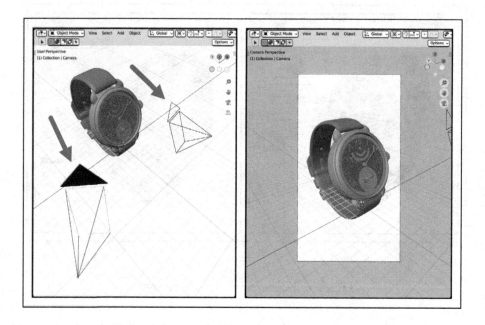

Figure 6.4 - *Active camera*

You can have several cameras in a scene, but only one of them will be active. The active camera will always show a filled triangle above their icon on the Viewport (Figure 6.4 - *Left*).

You can view what the active camera is currently framing using the Numpad 0 key. It will make you jump to the Camera view (Figure 6.4 - *Right*).

To make another camera active, select the camera object and press CTRL+Numpad 0. That makes any selected camera active. From the camera view, you can select the camera border and make adjustments to the framing:

– Press the G and R keys to move and rotate the camera

– Press the G key and Z key twice to make a dolly movement

When pressing G and the Z key twice, you will start a dolly movement, where it is possible to move the mouse cursor up and down to move forward and backward. The camera's local Z-axis always points towards the same direction it is currently viewing, which allows us to use those shortcuts.

By pressing an axis key twice, you will use the local coordinates for a transformation instead of global values.

6.2.1 Changing the camera focal length

Another way to control your framing for the camera is with the focal distance settings. With the camera object selected (1), go to the Object Data Properties tab (2) for viewing all camera options (Figure 6.5).

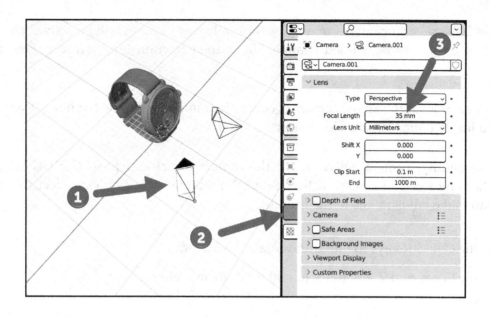

Figure 6.5 - Camera settings and focal length

At the camera settings, you will find the Focal length at the top (3). With the Focal length, we can change our camera's viewing angle from the scene.

Using the millimeters unit, you can get a broad view from the scene with focal distances of 16-20 mm (Figure 6.6). That is how we make a camera to have a wide or narrow view of the scene.

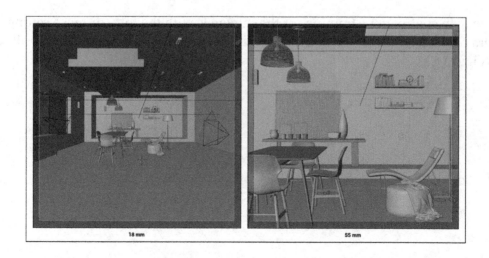

Figure 6.6 - Focal length difference - Left: 18mm - Right: 55mm

166

You have to keep in mind that using lower values for the focal distance might give you a wider view from the scene but will probably add some distortion to your render's borders.

6.2.2 Align the camera to view

Using transformation keys after selecting the camera might help you with an overall framing but will hardly help place the camera for render. The best way to align the camera for rendering is by using 3D Navigation shortcuts.

With the middle mouse button, you can orbit the scene and find a good viewing angle for a render. Once you get the best viewing angle, use a shortcut to align your active camera to that view. Press the CTRL+ALT+Numpad 0 keys.

By pressing those keys simultaneously, you align your active camera with the same viewing angle you have from the scene. It might not still be perfect, but you can make the final adjustments to get a perfect framing using transformation keys.

The option is also available from the **View** → **Align View** → **Align Active Camera to View** menu.

6.3 Rendering scenes

Now that you know how to align cameras in your scene and control viewing angles, it is time to start rendering scenes. To render in Blender, you can either press the F12 key or choose the **Render** → **Render Image** menu.

Once you start a render, you will see the image appearing in the output window. By using Eevee, results will appear in a couple of seconds. In the case of Cycles, it might take a few minutes to finish depending on several factors (Figure 6.7).

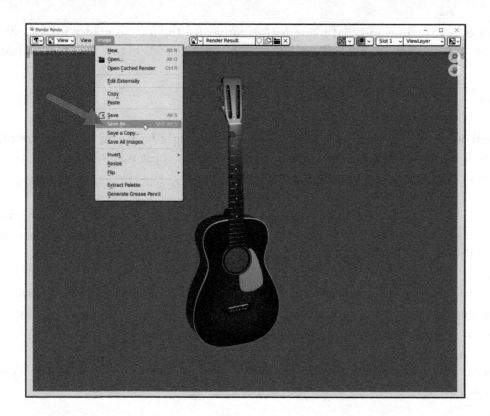

Figure 6.7 - *Render results*

The output window always shows what your active camera is currently viewing. If you want to cancel the render at any time, press the ESC key. It may take a while to stop your rendering, especially in Cycles, but it will eventually stop.

6.4 Saving a render

How to save your renders from the Output window in Blender? After having your render results showing in the Output window, use the **Image** menu to save it as an image file. Look for the "Save as…" to save a render (Figure 6.7).

A new window appears where it is possible to choose a location to save your render and also an image format. Here are the available options:

– PNG

– JPG

- TGA

- TIFF

- EXR

To always keep your render results with the highest possible quality, always save your projects as PNG files first. If you need a smaller version, you can convert the PNG to a JPG file later. Depending on your project, you might want to use EXR for post-processing. But, in most cases, a PNG is the best choice.

The reason to keep your renders as PNG files is because it uses a type of compression for images called *lossless*. With this method, you get larger file sizes but with no data loss from your renders. It is a compression similar to what ZIP containers do with text files.

On the other hand, a JPG file uses a compression method called *lossy*, which excludes some information to reduce file size. Every time you save a JPG file, the algorithm will exclude data from your image to reduce file size.

For that reason, try to save all renders as PNG files first and then convert them to JPG later if you need a smaller file.

6.4.1 Image settings for rendering

An important setting for any render in Blender is the resolution of your images, which is also a factor that can determine how long it will take for a render to finish. For instance, rendering an image with 300 x 200 pixels finishes a lot faster than a 4K image with 4096 x 2160 pixels.

Resolution settings are available in the Output Properties tab at the Properties Editor (Figure 6.8 - *Left*).

In the settings, you can manually type the size you wish to use for a render or get an industry-standard resolution from several presets (Figure 6.8 - *Right*).

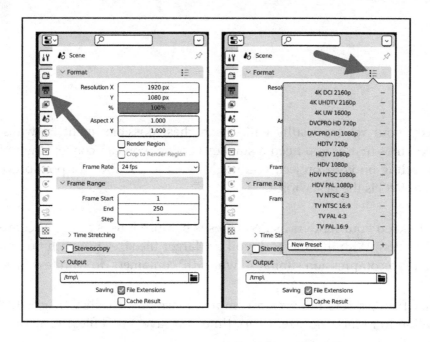

Figure 6.8 - Output and format settings

You can also choose your image format in the Output Properties tab and color settings. One of the benefits of using a PNG file besides the quality is using the RGBA color format. By using RGBA, you can have transparent pixels in your images (Figure 6.9 - *Left*).

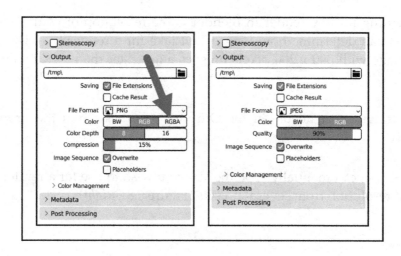

Figure 6.9 - Color settings for PNG and JPEG

That is useful to make renders with a transparent background. To render images with no background, go to the Film settings and enable an option called "Transparent" to make your renders appear with a transparent background. Having transparent pixels is useful to compose renders with other images. The option works for Cycles or Eevee (Figure 6.10).

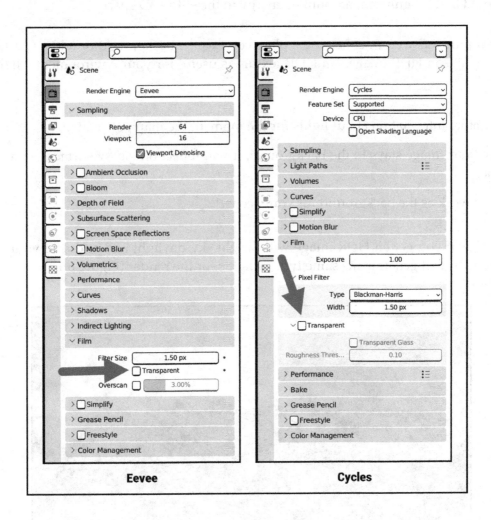

Figure 6.10 - *Transparent background for renders*

The JPG format used by Blender doesn't support transparent backgrounds, which will add a solid color instead of transparent pixels as a background in case you save the render results in JPG format.

6.5 Environmental lights

One of the first steps many artists take when starting to work on lights for a scene in Blender is to add an environmental light. That is a light coming from a scene's background, which could add a significant amount of energy to the entire 3D space.

For that purpose, we can either use a plain color as the background or add a special type of textures like an HDR image. An HDR texture is useful for your environmental lights because:

- They store information about lights for the moment the map got created.

- Since your image stays in the background, it will reflect on glossy surfaces across the scene.

- It may work as the background for your scene.

For instance, if you get an HDR image with bright sky daylight and add it to your scene's background, it will generate the same type of lights for the render (Figure 6.11).

Figure 6.11 - Daylight HDR

How to use an HDR in your background? Add an HDR in the World Properties tab at the Properties Editor (1). There you will find a field called Surface options. Press the "Use Nodes" button and go to the Color field (2). Click at the small button with a yellow circle on the left, and pick "Environment Texture" (3) (Figure 6.12).

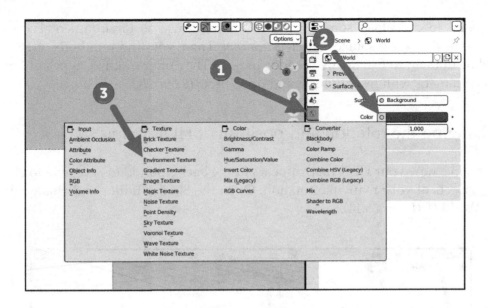

Figure 6.12 - *Adding an Environment Texture*

Once you add the Environment Texture to the Color, a small set of options appears with a button to open a file. Click at the "Open" button and get an HDR map from your computer or local network. It appears as your scene's background if you use the rendered shading mode (Figure 6.13).

Figure 6.13 - *HDR in the background*

173

If you want to download some free HDR maps to use as Environmental Textures in Blender, one of the best resources is *polyhaven.com*. There you find hundreds of HDR maps in the public-domain to use in any Blender project. They offer multiple types of lights and locations with maps with resolutions going up to 8K *(8192 pixels)*.

6.5.1 Changing the rotation and position of HDR maps

If you don't like how your HDR map appears in the background, it is possible to change all mapping aspects of your map, like rotation. Open the Shader Editor and change the View option to World (1)(Figure 6.14).

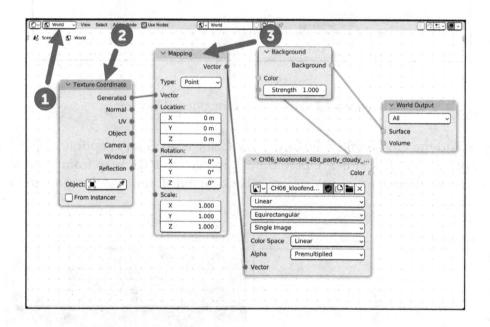

Figure 6.14 - *Shader Editor view*

It displays Nodes related to the World Properties tab, and the HDR map will be there for editing. Add the same Texture Coordinates (2) and Mapping (3) Nodes we used back in chapter 5.

Connect the Texture Coordinates and the Mapping to the Image Texture Node, and you will be able to control HDR rotation with the Rotation settings from the Mapping Node.

A few points regarding HDR maps for both Cycles and Eevee:

- In Cycles, you will get lights and shadows from HDR maps.

- Eevee can't cast shadows from HDR maps, which makes them less useful for real-time render.

- An HDR map might create different types of lighting. That depends on the location and timing used as a source for each HDR. Usually, you can get an idea about the lighting in the library's preview, where you download the HDR map.

When making changes to the location and rotation of HDR maps in Blender, use the Rendered shading mode. By using this shading mode in the 3D Viewport, you have real-time feedback of the HDR placement and can pick the best position and angle for your maps.

6.6 Illumination and types of lights

Environment lights will be a great help as a starting point for any project, but you will also need additional light sources. For instance, if you use Eevee for rendering, a light source will be the best choice to replace an HDR map since it can't cast shadows in real-time.

In Blender, you can create several types of lights with the SHIFT+A key (Figure 6.15).

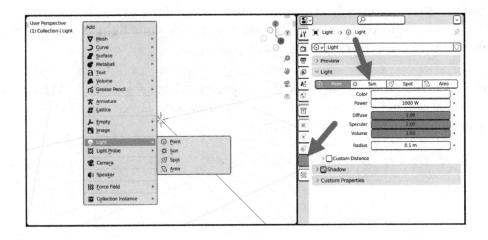

Figure 6.15 - *Lights options*

The list has options for lights includes:

- **Point**: Emit light from a single point in space in all directions.

– **Sun**: Simulate a distant light source that behaves like the Sun.

– **Spot**: A point that cast light in a cone shape.

– **Area**: A squared shape that emits lights from all the available shapes.

Each one of those lights has a purpose in a project. For instance, in a scene that tries to simulate daylight, you will probably use a Sun combined with an HDR map for a Cycles render.

It is possible to add each new lights using the SHIFT+A key or change an existing light source type by selecting it and opening the Object Data tab. There you will see buttons at the top where you can quickly swap between each type of light (Figure 6.16).

The Object Data tab also displays options regarding lights where you can control:

– Shadows

– Color

– Power

Besides those settings, you will also find contextual options for each light type. For instance, in the Area light options, you will set the size of your light plane. The Spot will show controls for a cone projection.

Options for each light also change based on your renderer selection. In Figure 6.16, you can see a comparison between settings for an *Area light* with Eevee and Cycles. Notice how they offer unique options based on each renderer.

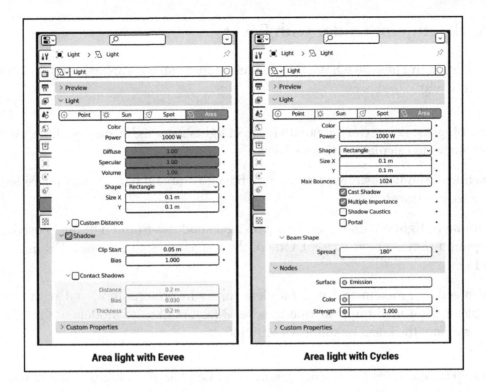

Figure 6.16 - *Comparing light settings with Eevee and Cycles*

You will see the most significant difference in the shadow settings with more options to control shadows when you select Eevee as a renderer.

6.7 Quick setup for rendering

Since each renderer requires specific settings to achieve good lighting results, we will use a simple scene to apply a quick setup using both Eevee and Cycles. In the process, we can tweak settings for lights and shadows.

From that scene, you will learn how to prepare a project for rendering with both engines.

Unfortunately, it is hard to replicate the same settings for all scenes in a 3D project. That happens because each scene has unique needs and aspects, which might demand adjustments from the author. However, you can use the following quick setup as a starting point for future projects and adapt each case's settings.

6.7.1 Quick setup for render with Eevee

To render a scene in Eevee, we have to consider a few details regarding renderer. You need special attention to:

- **Indirect Lights**: Eevee can't generate indirect lights from light sources alone. We have to use probes to calculate indirect bounces.

- **Reflections**: Another feature that you will have to emulate with probes are reflections from glossy surfaces.

- **Environment lights**: With Eevee, you won't get shadows from HDR maps used as the background (*Environment texture*). One of the best choices to replace HDR maps is an Area Light.

- **Light bleed**: A problem that you may encounter in projects rendered with Eevee is light bleed. That might appear due to several factors like 3D models with walls that don't have any thickness or shadows settings.

As a first step for the scene (Figure 6.17), you should add an Area Light that will work as an environment light. Since Eevee doesn't support shadow casting from HDR maps, an Area Light is a great option to use in the background.

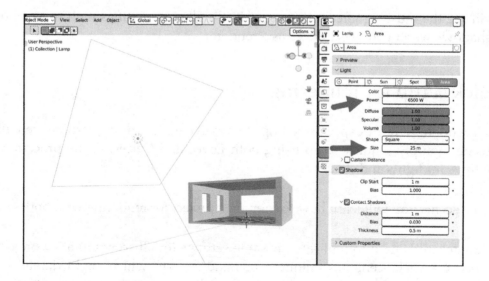

Figure 6.17 - *Area as the environmental light*

Using the rotation and move shortcuts, place the light source in the scene's background, far away from the model. Use the light settings to increase the size of that Area Light until it became larger than the model.

Enable Shadows and also Contact Shadows (Figure 6.17).

Besides an Area Light in the background, you can also add one Area Light to each of the windows to increase the scene's illumination. Use the size settings from the lights to adjust them to each Area Light (Figure 6.18). Scale them until they fit in each window.

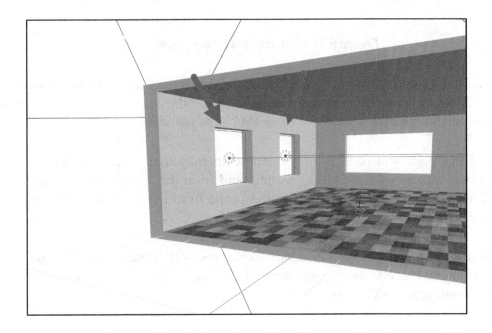

Figure 6.18 - *Area lights in windows*

Since Eevee can't handle indirect lights for rendering, we have to use a helper object for those calculations. The helper objects for Eevee have the name of Probes.

For indirect lights, you use a probe called Irradiance Volume. Press the SHIFT+A keys, and from the Light Probes group, add an Irradiance Volume. Select the Irradiance Volume and use the S key scale until it covers the entire scene (1)(2) (Figure 6.19).

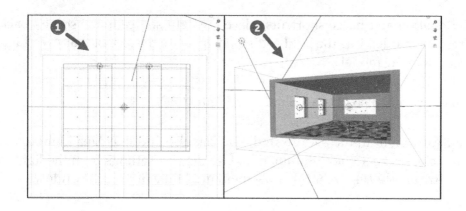

Figure 6.19 - *Irradiance Volume in the scene*

The Irradiance Volume has a box-like shape, and it identifies an area where Eevee will later process indirect light bounces. Only what is inside the Probe volume receives indirect light bounces. You can add as many of those Probes as you need.

The next probe we will need is a Reflection Cubemap that captures reflections and cast them in glossy surfaces. Press SHIFT+A again and from the Light Probes group, add a Reflection Cubemap. Using the G key, raise the probe from the ground level and place it in your scene's middle.

Unlike an Irradiance Volume with a box-like shape, a Reflection Cubemap has a default shape of a sphere. Use a scale transformation to increase your probe's size until it becomes bigger than your scene (1)(2)(Figure 6.28).

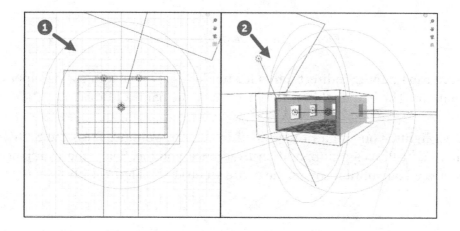

Figure 6.20 - *Reflection Cubemap*

It is time to use the settings from the Render tab in the Properties Editor. Locate the Indirect Lighting settings (1) and press Bake Indirect Lighting (2). It starts to calculate indirect lights and reflections for all Probes (Figure 6.21).

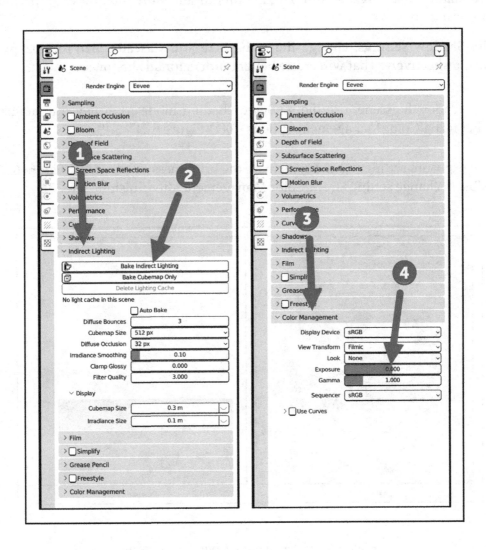

Figure 6.21 - Indirect lights baking

You will see a progress bar at the bottom of your interface. It can take a couple of seconds or minutes to process all Probes, which depends on your scene's complexity.

We can make additional enhancements to the scene by:

– **Enable Ambient Occlusion**: That will generate contact shadows.

- **Enable Screen Space Reflections**: To create reflections based on a mirror image of your scene.

- **In the Shadows settings, enable High Bitdepth and Soft Shadows**: To increase all shadows' quality.

- **In the Shadow settings, change the Cube Size and Cascade Size for 1024px and 2048px, respectively**: That will create better borders for all shadows.

Before you render the scene, use the rendered shading mode from Eevee to adjust lights even further using Color Management options (3)(4)(Figure 6.21).

With the exposure settings, you can increase the brightness of the scene (Figure 6.22). It is also possible to change settings from Color Management after finishing a render.

Figure 6.22 - *Exposure settings comparison*

If you press the F12 key after using all those settings, you will get the Eevee's rendered image at the Output Window.

The workflow is a basic guide on how to prepare any scene to render in real-time. It may not be the most accurate visualization of a scene regarding realism, but it is fast. It might not work for all types of projects, but you can use it as a starting point.

Tip: Use the settings from the Output tab to choose the resolution for your render images.

6.7.2 Quick setup for render with Cycles

Unlike Eevee, you can use a more direct approach with Cycles, and it doesn't require any type of probe to calculate indirect lights. However, you might have to wait a little longer for the render to finish.

The first thing you must do is to set the current render as Cycles in the Render settings. For a daylight simulation with Cycles, use two types of lights; *Sun Light* and *Area Lights*.

The first one will be a Sun Light that you placed in a location where you want to simulate the Sun position (1). Also, enable shadows in the Sun settings and change the Angle value to a number close to zero like "0.05" to get hard edge shadows (2) (Figure 6.23).

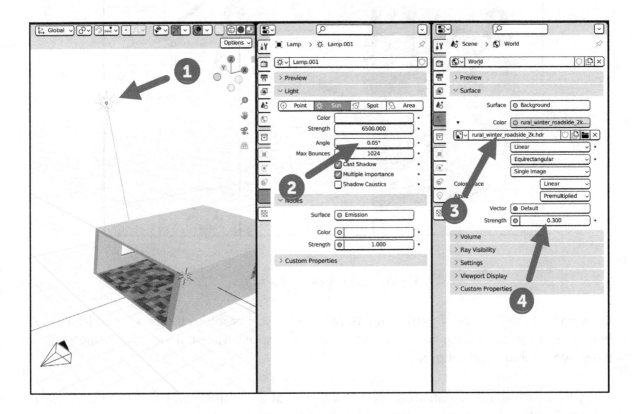

Figure 6.23 - Sun and HDR settings

With Cycles, we can use an HDR map for environmental light to give an initial boost in the scene lighting. Go to the World tab and add an HDR map to the background (3). Adjust your HDR map's power level in *Strength field* (4), and we can move on to the next step.

Tip: You can also use the R key to rotate the Sun and find a location where the light beams will more efficiently enter your scene.

In some cases, using a Sun Light with HDR maps won't add the necessary energy to the scene. For that reason, we need a second source. Using Area lights in each window will also help with that type of project (1). Disable shadow casting (2) for those lights and also scale each Area Light until they fit the same size of each window (1)(Figure 6.24).

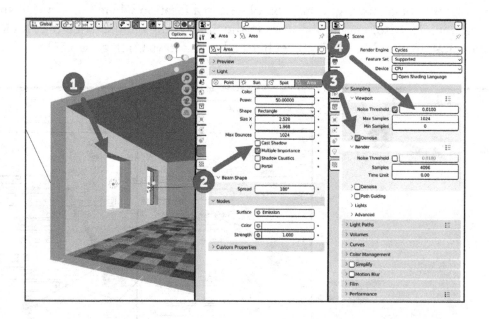

Figure 6.24 - Area light settings

As part of the process of getting lights with the best possible settings, you will have to play with the *Power settings* for all sources to find the appropriate balance. The same values won't work for all types of projects.

If you use the Rendered Shading mode for Cycles at this point, you will have a great idea of Eevee's differences. The render progress displays a slow evolution, starting with a grainy image that stops before 1024 interactions. We can test the visualization of this scene using a Max Samples of 1024 and keep the Noise Threshold as 0.1, as displayed in Figure 6.24 (4).

The Noise Threshold controls how close we go to the Max Samples value in a render. You can disable this setting to use the full value of Max Samples, which will take more time to process.

Enable the Denoise option below Sampling settings (3) Figure 6.24. As a result, we get a render preview of the scene with all light sources (Figure 6.25). How to get a render Preview? Use the shading modes from the 3D Viewport and choose *Rendered*.

Figure 6.25 - Render preview with Cycles

Those interactions (Sampling) in Cycles have a limit that you can adjust at the Render tab, with a combination of Noise Threshold and Max Samples.

Tip: You can interrupt the render for your preview using the pause button next to the shading modes selector.

6.7.3 Rendering with the GPU

One of the biggest challenges to render a scene in Cycles is finding an optimal sample limit that will give you a noiseless image. Usually, a value between 500 and 1000 gives you good results, but it depends on several factors. The difference in render times from 500 to 1000 samples could be a few minutes or hours.

The total render time for this particular render was 11 seconds, using the GPU to speed up the process.

It is possible to select your graphics-card to process a scene from Cycles in the Device field (Render tab). If you don't see the GPU option, go to the **Edit → Preferences** menu, and open the System tab (1). There you have a list with the Cycles Render Devices (2)(Figure 6.26).

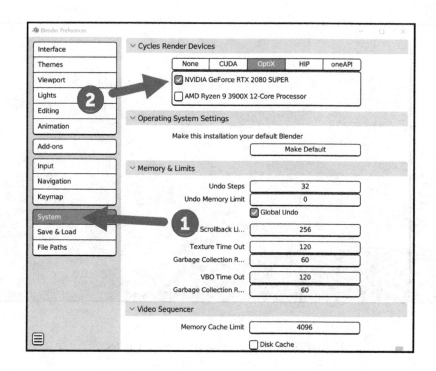

Figure 6.26 - Using GPU to speedup renders

For Radeon cards from AMD, you must select the HIP field, and for NVIDIA, you can use either CUDA or OptiX. For Intel cards, we have the oneAPI option.

The CUDA option will already add a huge boost to your renders, and for maximum speed, you can enable OptiX. However, not all features from Cycles are compatible with OptiX. If you have a Mac with Apple Silicon, it is possible to use Metal and access the GPU of your processor (M1 or M2 processors in all variants).

After enabling the GPU for rendering, you can select the device from the list. You can select the GPU for rendering in the Render tab (1)(Figure 6.27).

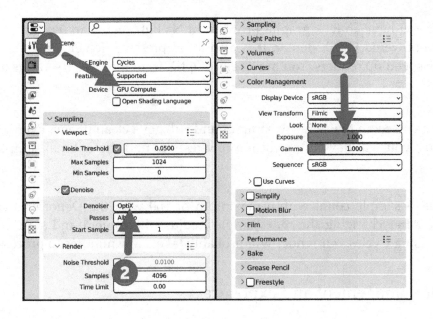

Figure 6.27 - *Choosing the GPU and exposure settings*

In any case, you should use the GPU if you have one available on the computer used for render. Just remember that your scene must fit in the VRAM space for processing. Otherwise, you will have to use the CPU only.

6.7.4 Denoiser tool with fewer samples

To help you using fewer samples for a faster render, we can always use the Denoiser tool in Cycles. Go to the Sampling options and enable the Denoiser tool if you are not using it already. Below your Sampling settings, you can enable the Denoiser for either the Render or Viewport. The Viewport option removes noise from a render preview (2)(Figure 6.27).

The Denoiser applies a "blur" filter for a render that will remove a considerable amount of noise from renders. It is not a perfect solution but helps a lot in reducing render times.

You can also choose from three different types of methods for Denoising:

– **NLM:** The standard method to remove noise from renders.

– **OpenImageDenoise:** Here, we have a powerful denier filter that uses machine learning to removes noise from an image.

– **OptiX:** If you have an RTX graphics-card from NVIDIA, you can use the artificial intelligence-powered OptiX denier. It is also an impressive denier filter that can dramatically speed up renders. You must select OptiX from the Cycles settings to use this method.

That will give you room to use fewer samples and still get a clean image. Even with the Denoiser options, you will have to perform a few tests to find the optimal sample value for your project.

In our case, a sample count with a maximum of 500 with the Denoiser enabled gives good results. After changing the max samples, adjust the camera and start your render. Since we are using Cycles, our render will probably take a few minutes to process.

6.7.5 Color management and exposure

After you render the project, it is time to make adjustments to your scene's brightness with the Color Management options (3)(Figure 6.27).

It is possible to change your render looks using options from the Color Management field, even after a render ended. It might give you a lot of flexibility to tweak lights and also color settings. Use the exposure settings to get a brighter result for the image (Figure 6.28).

Figure 6.28 - Exposure results

Save the render results to disk, and you have a scene rendered in Cycles.

What is next?

In the realm of 3D modeling, many project components often involve retracing steps and consistently employing tools to shape intricate models. However, rendering and lighting deviate from this pattern, necessitating a bespoke touch for every scene.

Such an approach is essential due to the distinctive characteristics inherent to each project —varying scales, material configurations, and contextual elements. Consequently, fine-tuning becomes paramount for each fresh scene. Over time, you'll come to appreciate that numerous scenes can conveniently align with shared environmental lighting and material settings.

Contrastingly, when it's about setting up lights, adjustments remain an ever-present requisite for every scene, inclusive of sampling value alterations.

Your surest ally in mastering rendering? Undoubtedly, it's hands-on practice. A productive exercise involves analyzing a photograph and attempting to mirror its ambiance and shading patterns using Blender's arsenal.

Transitioning from our rendering discourse, Chapter 7 will usher you into the captivating world of animation. Leveraging Blender's prowess, immerse yourself in the art of keyframe integration to animate a spectrum of movements.

Chapter 7 - Animation and motion with Blender

Did you know that even when you're rendering a solitary image in Blender, you're actually dabbling with animation? At its core, Blender is crafted to generate animations, boasting an array of features and instruments for motion graphics.

In this chapter, we'll guide you on crafting animations anchored in a fundamental concept: the keyframe. Keyframes enable us to timestamp a specific property within the animation. Essential to animation is the presence of objects marked with multiple keyframes on a Timeline. This paves the way for us to engage with a process known as interpolation.

Here is a list of what you will learn in this chapter:

– How animations work in Blender

– Controlling and managing frames and length for animations

– Add/Remove and manage keyframes

– Creating simple animations with keyframes

– Making linear animations using curves

7.1 How to make an animation with Blender?

The method Blender uses to create animations has a name of interpolation, which works based on a combination of keyframes and transformations along a Timeline. Each keyframe "marks" a property of an object at a certain point in time. You can think of an animation as a sequence of still images. When using a certain speed to reproduce them, you have the illusion of motion. Each still image in animation has a name of frame.

An interpolation animation uses the different values of a property to create motion. For instance, if an animation has 50 frames where you set a property with a value of 200 at frame 1, and a value of 500 at frame 50.

The interpolation method calculates a proportional progression between frames 2 and 49. With a minimum of two keyframes in a sequence, if you hit the play button, we visualize an interpolation between the first and second keyframes.

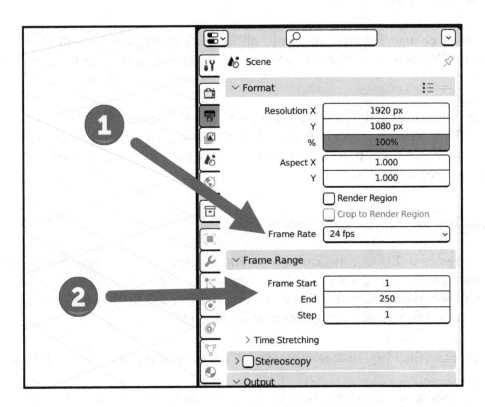

Figure 7.1 - *Frame rate and range settings*

A Timeline for animations uses frames to identify the time. Usually, an animation has 24 to 30 frames for one second of animation. For instance, if you get an animation that has 5 seconds with 30 frames per second requires 150 frames.

The rate of frames displayed per second has a name of *frame rate*, and it appears in lots of places with the acronym FPS. For the rest of the book, we will use FPS to identify frame rates.

By default, you always start with an FPS of 24, which you can change at the Output tab (1) (Figure 7.1).

For video and animation, most artists use either 24 or 30 FPS. Since animations can also consume many resources, Blender limits the total length with a start and end frames. Below the frame rate settings, you can set the start and end frames in your current scene (2).

Those values always start with 1 and 250 for start and end, respectively. If you have to create an animation with 3 seconds using a 30 FPS, which requires 90 frames, you can keep the start to 1 and set the end to 90.

If you don't change the start and end, all animations in Blender will occur between frames 1 and 250. You can still create a 90 frames animation and don't touch the start and end frames.

However, when hitting the play button to preview your motion, it will go from frame 1 to 250, even with motion stopping at frame 90. That is also true for rendering. Instead of rendering 90 frames, you will process 250. Always change the start and end frames according to your project requirements.

7.1.1 Adding keyframes to objects

To add keyframes in Blender, we can use several methods from keyboard shortcuts to the Context menu. No matter the way used to create keyframes, you won't be able to make animations without them. After selecting an object, you can use the I key to add a keyframe. That is the easiest way to add keyframes to anything in Blender.

Once you press the I key, a list with all available keyframe types appears (1) (Figure 7.2).

You must choose the keyframe type based on the kind of animation data needed for a project. The keyframe type has a direct relation to the property you are animating.

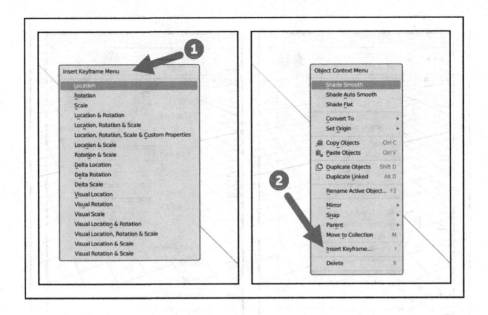

Figure 7.2 - *Keyframe types and Context Menu*

For instance, if you are trying to animate a rotation, you will create a keyframe using the Rotation keyframe type. In case you want to make a rotation and scale animation at the same time, you can use the RotScale keyframe type. The keyframe type selection only appears when you are creating keyframes in the 3D Viewport.

Another way to insert keyframes to objects is with a right-click on the 3D Viewport. Using the Context menu, you can choose "Insert keyframe..." to add keyframes (2) (Figure 7.2).

By the way, always create keyframes in *Object Mode* for animation!

It is also possible to add keyframes in the 3D Viewport Sidebar, or using the Object tab at the Properties Editor. If you right-click at any property like a location, you will see keyframe options (1) (Figure 7.3).

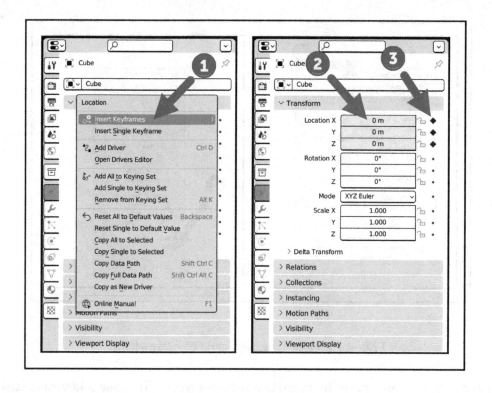

Figure 7.3 - *Inserting keyframes in properties*

For instance, if you right-click at the X Location field:

- **Insert keyframes**: Creates a keyframe for all three axes in the location property.
- **Insert Single Keyframe**: Adds a keyframe only to the X location property.

By using the right-click at single option properties, you won't have to choose keyframe types. You will have to choose whether adding the keyframe to a single property or all three (X, Y, and Z-axis). That depends on the type of animation you need.

After adding a keyframe to those properties, a yellow background appears at the property editor (2). That is a visual code showing a keyframe that exists at that property in the current frame. On the right, notice that a diamond-shaped symbol appears instead of the small dot available in all properties (3) (Figure 7.3).

Another way to add keyframes to any object is by clicking at those dots, which will make the diamond shape icon appear. It identifies an existing keyframe for that property.

Info: *The interpolation process uses the keyframes to create animations. It takes the difference in properties between two keyframes to generate all intermediate values automatically.*

7.1.2 Removing and updating keyframes

What if you want to remove a keyframe? You can easily remove and manage keyframes with a right-click on a property value that has a keyframe. If you right-click, a menu with several options to manage keyframes appears (Figure 7.4).

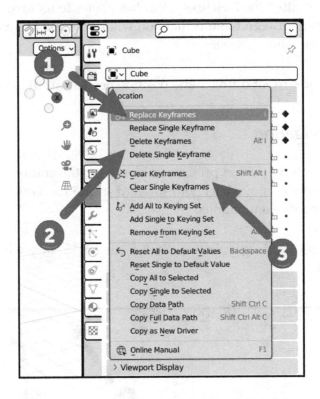

Figure 7.4 - Managing keyframes

There is more than one option to manage keyframes:

– **Replace keyframes**: Updates all keyframes' property value and keeps them in the same locations in time. (1)

– **Replace Single Keyframe**: Changes the value of your selected keyframe for that particular moment in time. (1)

- **Delete Keyframes**: Removes all keyframes from the object for that specific property in a single frame. (2)

- **Delete Single Keyframe**: Excludes only the selected keyframe for that frame. (2)

- **Clear Keyframes**: Removes all keyframes in all properties for the entire Timeline. (3)

- **Clear Single keyframes**: Removes all keyframes for the property selected in all Timeline. (3)

Notice that you can use either the Delete or Clear keyframes to remove animation data from an object. The difference between them is that you will remove keyframes for a single frame (*Delete*) or the entire animation (*Clear*).

Make sure you set the current frame in the position needed to edit a particular keyframe!

7.1.3 Timeline navigation

An essential tool for your animation projects in Blender is the ability to navigate the Timeline. Once you learn how to move back and forward inside the Timeline Editor, it will become much easier to manage animations.

The first thing to do is identify how to set a current frame, which will help insert keyframes for properties.

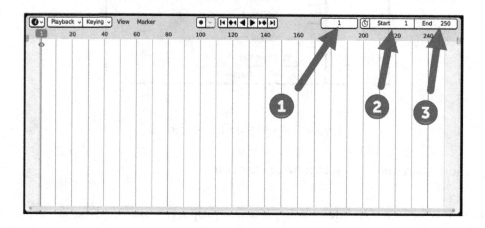

Figure 7.5 - Timeline Editor

In the 3D Viewport, you will find the current frame from your animation on your screen's top left. It appears next to the name of your active Collection. Using the Timeline Editor, you will also be able to see the current frame at the top right (1), and also set the start (2) and end (3) frames (Figure 7.5).

A few shortcuts you will want to use for animation control:

- **SPACEBAR**: Play the animation.

- **LEFT ARROW**: Jump one frame backward.

- **RIGHT ARROW**: Jump one frame forward.

- **UP ARROW**: Jump to the next keyframe.

- **DOWN ARROW**: Jump to the previous keyframe.

- **SHIFT+LEFT ARROW**: Jump to the start frame.

- **SHIFT+RIGHT ARROW**: Jump to the end frame.

You can also navigate the Timeline using the playback head, which is the vertical blue line marking the current frame. Using the left mouse button, you can click and drag that line to change the current frame.

That same line appears in several other animation related editors, like the Graph Editor and the Dope sheet.

Tip: The shortcuts used at the Timeline Editor also works on all other animation related Editors.

7.2 Creating a simple animation

Now that we know how to create keyframes and navigate in the Timeline Editor, it is possible to create a simple animation. The purpose of the animation is to make an object move in the 3D Viewport. You can use any object as an example of the animation.

In our case, we can grab a text object created using the SHIFT+A keys and choosing the Text option. To edit the text contents, go to Edit Mode with the text selected, and replace it as if you were in a text editor.

For the animation, we can use the following data:

- **Length**: 2 seconds
- **FPS**: 30
- **Start frame**: 1 (2)
- **End frame**: 60 (3)

Change most of the settings for this animation in the Timeline Editor. Only the FPS requires the Output tab at the Properties Editor to update from 24 to 30 the frame rate.

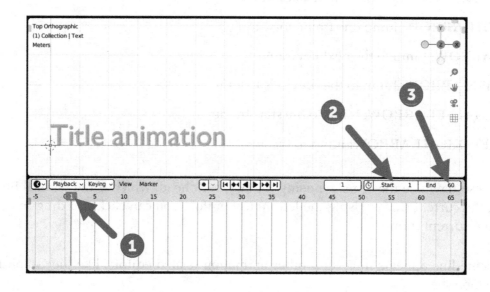

Figure 7.6 - *Animation start settings*

Tip: *You can press the Home key to adjust the zoom of your Timeline editor after setting the Start and End frames.*

Our animation subject starts on the left side of our 3D Viewport and move to the right. The animation uses location keyframes only. Select the object you want to animate and make sure frame 1 is your current frame (1) (Figure 7.6).

Press the I key and choose a location keyframe. You can also use the Sidebar or the Object tab in the Properties Editor to add keyframes. There you will right-click above the Location field and choose Insert Keyframes.

The Timeline Editor now displays a diamond-shaped icon for the selected object in frame 1 (1) (Figure 7.7). Notice that the object name and active Collection will also turn to yellow, indicating a keyframe (2). Those names appear at the top left your 3D Viewport.

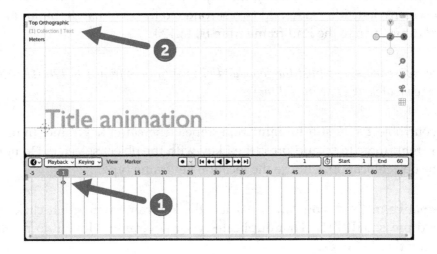

Figure 7.7 - Timeline with keyframe

Move the current frame to 60 (1) and keep the text object selected. Press the G key and move your 3D object to the right (2). Once the 3D object is on the right side, press the I key, and choose location again. A new keyframe appears in the Timeline (3) (Figure 7.8).

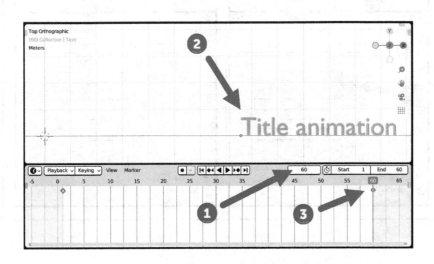

Figure 7.8 - Second keyframe

To start and preview animations, press the SPACEBAR key or the play button in the Timeline. That starts playing any animation you have in all Editors.

We can expand the animation, making the object stay still for one second and then going back to your screen's left side. First, add two seconds to the total length of our animation. In the Timeline Editor, change the End frame from 60 to 120.

Tip: Use the mouse wheel to adjust the zoom and view all frames from 1 to 120. The Home key can also adjust the zoom of your Timeline Editor.

To make your object stay still in animation, repeat the same keyframe. In our case, you can set the current frame to 90 and press the I key with the object selected. Do not make any changes to the object location. Choose the location keyframe type.

As an alternative method, you can also select the keyframe with a left-click at the Timeline Editor and press SHIFT+D. That duplicates your keyframe. Move it to position 90 and confirm with another left-click.

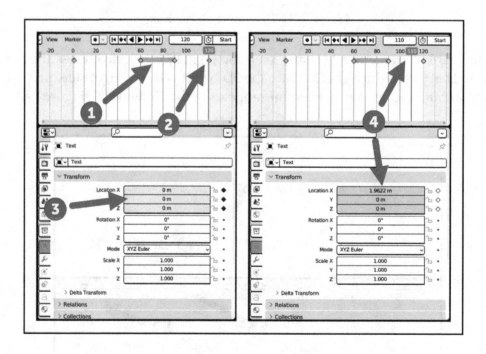

Figure 7.9 - *Timeline with solid lines*

You will notice that from frames 60 to 90, a solid line appears connecting both keyframes in the Timeline (1) (Figure 7.9).

That is a visual representation of two keyframes with no changes between properties. Since we didn't move the object, it has the same location value for both keyframes.

Go to frame 120 and move your object to the left side of your screen. Once there, press the I key and choose the location keyframe type again (2). Press the SPACEBAR key, and you will see the object starting in the left and moving to the right. After staying still for one second, it will go back to the left side.

Besides the solid line connecting two keyframes that shares the same data, you will also find other places displaying animation data color codes. In the Sidebar and Object tab properties with a (Figure 7.9):

- **Yellow background**: means an existing keyframe at the current frame (3)
- **Green background**: Value created by interpolation between two keyframes (4)

Using those color codes helps to identify when animation data exists in any property.

When you are in a frame where the selected object has a keyframe, your property displays a yellow background. For the intermediate frames where interpolation is occurring, the property background will be green.

7.3 Managing animation timing

You might want to make changes to the timing and speed of your animations in Blender after evaluating a project. To make such adjustments, you have to move keyframes back and forward for timing adjustments.

For instance, if you take the animation created in section 7.2, we can perform timing adjustments straight in the Timeline Editor. There you can select each keyframe, and with the G key moves them around.

By making two keyframes closer to each other, you make any animation faster. If you increase the distance between them, a slower animation is the outcome (Figure 7.10).

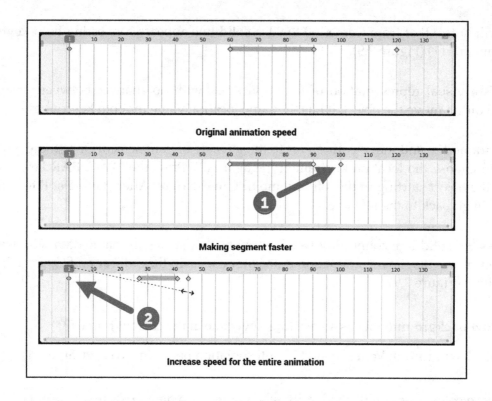

Original animation speed

Making segment faster

Increase speed for the entire animation

Figure 7.10 - *Timing adjustments for keyframes*

To manipulate keyframes in the Timeline or any other editor in Blender, use the same selection keys and transformations from 3D modeling projects.

If you want to adjust the entire animation timing, a scale transformation is the best choice. Press the A key to select all keyframes and use the S key to scale up or down animation as the whole.

By using a scale transformation, you must be careful with the current frame. That frame works as the pivot point for the scale. To keep your animation starting in the same frame, make sure you set the current frame as the first one from your animation, before pressing the S key. Notice that in Figure 7.10, I have the current frame as one during the scale transformation.

Using any other frame as the current frame during a scale might completely change your animation's Start and End frames.

Tip: *You can also use the Snap at the Timeline Editor. Select a keyframe and press SHIFT+S to show options related to animation.*

7.4 Controlling animation with curves

If you take a close look at the animation created in section 7.2, notice that it's not linear. The object gains speed in the beginning and slows down by the end of each period of animation. That type of motion for animations has the name of easing.

Any interpolation animation created in Blender uses easing for motion regardless of the property. To view and edit that type of animation data, we can use the Graph Editor, which shows a visual representation of all motion as curves (Figure 7.11).

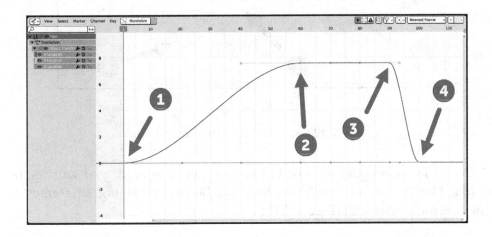

Figure 7.11 - Graph Editor

Change the Timeline Editor in the interface to a Graph Editor, using the Editor Type selector.

There you will see a lot more information about animations than what is available at the Timeline. For instance, you will be able to see individual animation channels on the left. Some controls to lock animations (padlock icon) and hide curves from the editor (checkbox icon).

The graphs display animation data using the horizontal axis for the frames and vertical axis for the property values.

Use the same zoom controls to adjust the viewing of your curves. With the Home key, you can fit all curves and keyframes in the current editor. If your keyboard doesn't have a Home key, use the **View → Frame All** menu.

The keyframes appear as small dots at the start and end of each curve (1) (Figure 7.12).

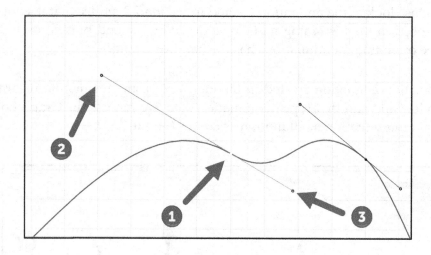

Figure 7.12 - Keyframes in the Graph Editor

If you select a keyframe and use the G key to move it around, you will see the curve structure adjusting to the new keyframe location. Besides changing keyframes, you will also see the control handlers (2) (Figure 7.12).

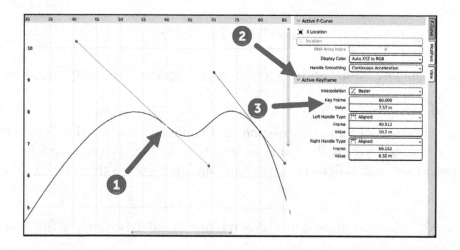

Figure 7.13 - Keyframe values

By selecting the handlers, you can deform the curve and change the animation's speed and easing.

Another option to edit animation data inside the Graph Editor is with the Sidebar. With a keyframe selected (1), you can press the N key to open the Sidebar for the Graph Editor and change the values for that particular keyframe (2) (Figure 7.13).

At the Key field (3), you can change the frame and also the value for the property that has a keyframe. It is an easy way to make changes to any keyframe.

To remove any easing from the animation, you can change the Interpolation Modes. In the Graph Editor, press the A key to select all keyframes and go to the **Key → Interpolation Mode** menu. There you will choose the **Linear** option.

That changes your curves to straight lines, which will turn the motion to a linear progression with no easing (Figure 7.14).

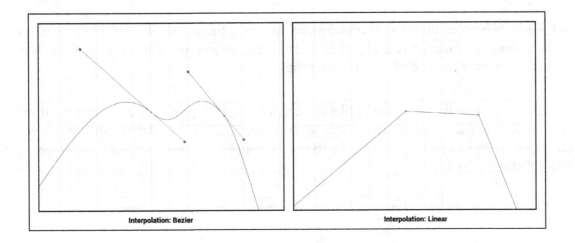

Figure 7.14 - *Linear motion*

Regarding animation, always use easing when you want to create natural movement, and for artificial motion, like machines, use the linear interpolation.

7.5 Hierarchies for animations

For animation projects that demand multiple objects interacting with each other, an option that can create hierarchical relations between 3D models will become useful. That tool allows an animator to create a movement based on a parenting relation between objects.

In Blender, you create hierarchies for animation using the CTRL+P keys to parenting objects. To make it easier to understand, we can name two objects in a hierarchy as parent and child:

- **Parent**: Object that can receive transformations and will replicate all of them to the children.

- **Child**: Object that inherits all transformations from the parent. If you rotate or move the parent, all children will also receive the same animation. However, any transformation applied to the child won't affect the parent.

For instance, if we have a 3D model like the one shown in Figure 7.15, we can make it work as a robotic arm. All we have to do is adjust the correct parenting relation between each object. Select the child first (1) followed by the parent object (2), and press CTRL+P to create a relation between them.

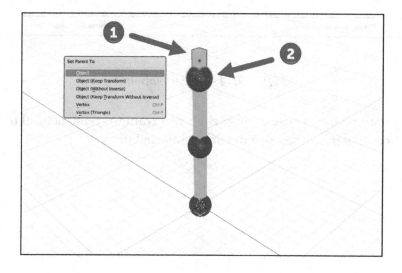

Figure 7.15 - Objects for robotic arm

For a full robotic arm motion, use the object near the base as the main parent for all structures. To create a parenting relation, you must select at least two objects. The last object selected (*Active Object*) will always be the parent.

Suppose you make a mistake, press ALT+P to break the connection. How to verify the parenting? Simple, select the parent, and apply a rotation. You will see the child object following the same rotation from a parent.

All child objects follow transformations from their parents. Repeat the parenting process for the remaining parts of the model, according to Figure 7.16.

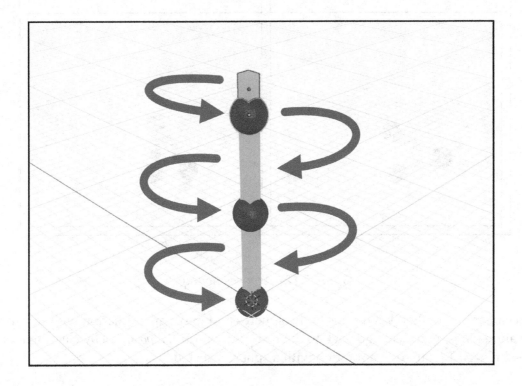

Figure 7.16 - Parenting structure

After you have the full model with parenting relations, an arm's animation becomes a lot easier. By selecting the base sphere of the object, you will move and rotate the entire arm. Select the spheres and apply individual rotations to create poses for the arm (Figure 7.17).

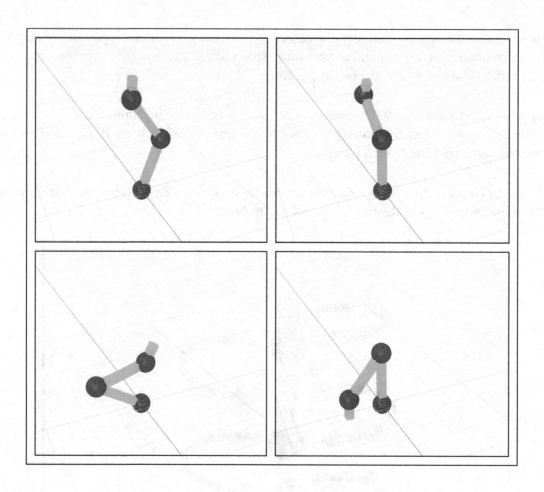

Figure 7.17 - Arm positioning

You can apply rotation keyframes to the spheres and make an animation with the arm. In those animations, you easily go back to the rest position (*Initial position*) by clearing all rotations—Press ALT+R to reset a rotation with a sphere selected.

Use the ALT key with any transformation shortcut to return the object property to their original value. The same option is also available from the **Object** → **Clear** menu.

7.6 Constraints for animations

In animation projects, you might want to use a special type of tool that will help to create motion with interactions between objects. The constraints can add certain rules to animated objects, making a few types of projects a lot easier.

To add a constraint, you have to select a 3D object first (1). You will find them in the Properties Editor in the Object Constraint tab (2). Click at the *Add Object Constraint* to see the full list of options available for your selection (3) (Figure 7.18).

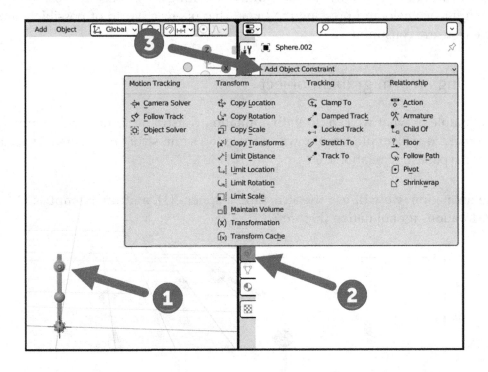

Figure 7.18 - Object constraint

After adding a constraint to an object, you will have unique options for each constraint type. The panel works like options from modifiers, where you can manage and reorder constraints applied to any selected object.

Among constraint types available, you will find:

- **Copy Location, Copy Rotation, and Copy Scale**: Makes the selected object using the same transformation data from the target object.

- **Limit Location, Limit Rotation, and Limit Scale**: Makes the object chosen to receive a limit for each transformation based on a target object.

- **Child of**: You can create parenting relations that can receive keyframes.

A key component of all constraints is the Influence option. With the influence, it is possible to set how each constraint affects object motion. An influence of 1 means it has a 100% impact on the motion. By dropping that value to zero, it is possible to "turn off" a constraint.

You can easily add keyframes to the influence settings, by placing the mouse cursor above the influence field and pressing the I key. That opens a world of possible animations we can create using constraints.

7.6.1 Making an arm grab an object

An easy example of what we can do with animation constraints is making an arm grab an object. To make our example simple, we can use the same structure created in section 7.5 with the same parenting relations.

For the animation, we will use the structure, a sphere (1), and three empties (2)(3)(4) to mark key locations for animation (Figure 7.19).

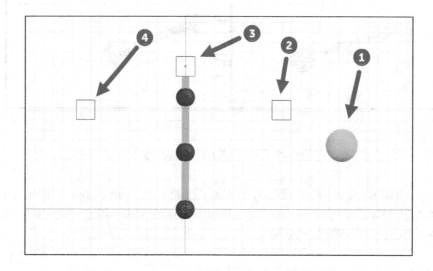

Figure 7.19 - Scene for animation

The objective is to make our structure grab the sphere and release it on the opposite side. It is a simple animation, which would require a lot of work to create without constraints.

Before we start, set all objects relations using the parenting tool. The empty close to our arm's tip must be a child of the object at the top (3)(Figure 7.19), named "hand." Select the empty first and then the "hand." Press CTRL+P to create a parenting relation.

Info: You will see a dashed line connecting the Empty and "hand" once they have a parenting relation.

Using the F2 key to rename all empties with the following names (Figure 7.19):

– **Empty near the sphere (2)**: firstEmpty

– **Empty near the "hand" (3)**: armEmpty

– **Empty on the right (4)**: endEmpty

Our animation will have 120 frames and an FPS of 30. Press the R key, to apply rotations and bend the arm:

– **From frame 1 to 30**: Rotate the arm close to the "firstEmpty."

– **From frame 31 to 90**: Rotate the arm to the other side, close to the "endEmpty."

– **From frame 91 to 120**: Rotate the arm away from the "endEmpty."

The animation occurs only in the sphere objects, and to clear your motion between frames 90 and 120, you can press ALT+R at frame 120.

By pressing the SPACEBAR key, you will see the arm moving in the 3D Viewport, but the sphere remains in the same location.

Now, select the sphere object (1) and apply three "Copy Location" constraints (2). In each constraint, choose as the target object one of the empties (3)(5)(7). Change the influence of the constraints with the "endEmpty" and "armEmpty" to zero (6)(8)(Figure 7.20).

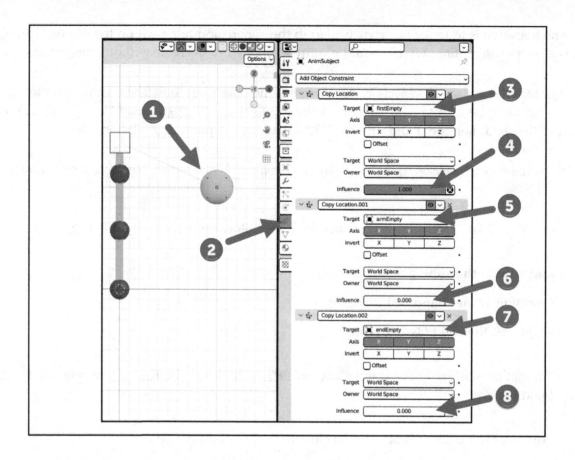

Figure 7.20 - Constraints for sphere

The influence for the Copy Location with a target set to the firstEmpty remains as 1 (4).

Make sure your current frame is 1 and apply a keyframe to all influences (1). You can either right-click on each property and choose "Insert keyframe..." or place the mouse cursor above each influence and press the I key (2)(3)(4) (Figure 7.21).

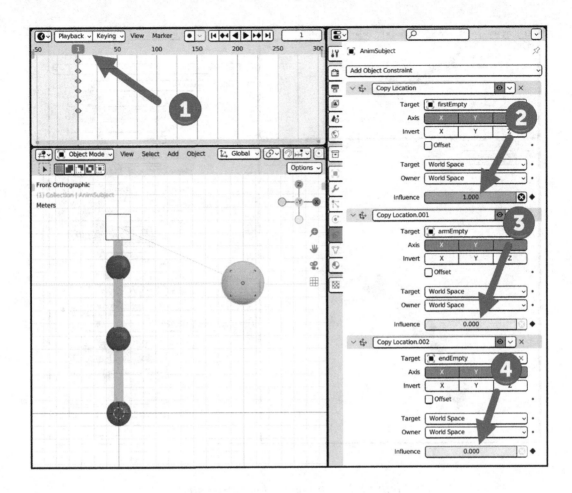

Figure 7.21 - *Keyframes for constraints*

Remember that you can add keyframes to any property in Blender using the same procedure. Place the mouse cursor above a property and press the I key.

Go to frame 30 and insert keyframes to all of the influences again. In frame 31, when your arm gets closer to the sphere, change the influences (1). Change the influence to zero for the constraint with "firstEmpty" as a target (2) and one for the "armEmpty" constraint (3)(Figure 7.22).

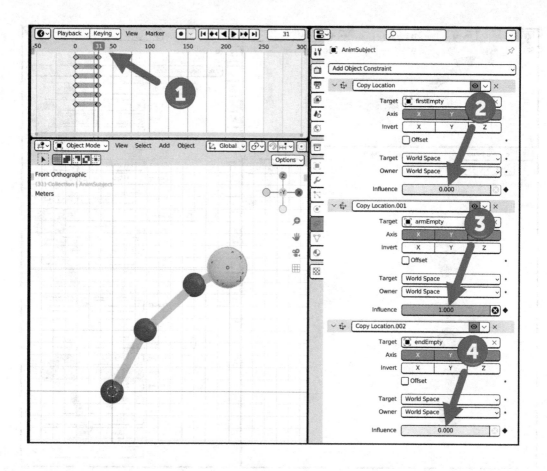

Figure 7.22 - Influences for constraints

Apply keyframes to all constraint influences again (2)(3)(4). By previewing your animation, you see that the arm will "grab" the sphere in frame 31. From that point forward, the sphere follows any movement of the arm.

Go to frame 90 and apply keyframes to all influences in the three constraints. In frame 91 (1), change the constraint's influence with the "armEmpty" as the target to zero (3) and the "endEmpty" to one (4). Apply keyframes to all of the constraint influences (2)(3)(4) (Figure 7.23).

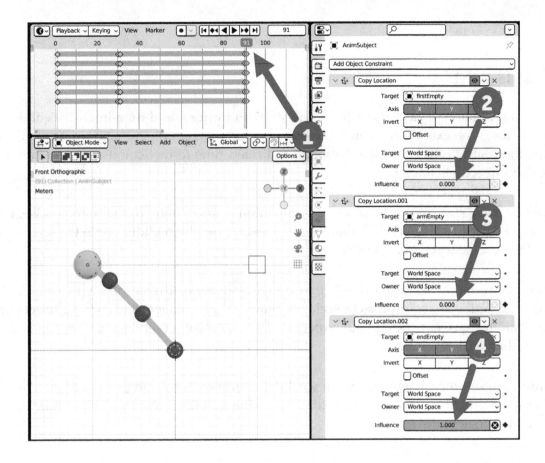

Figure 7.23 - *Last keyframes*

If you preview your animation, the arm moves until it grabs the sphere at frame 31. Our structure bends and rotates towards the opposite side, carrying the sphere. In the end, it releases the object on the left side of your 3D Viewport, at frame 91.

That is just one example of what we can do with constraints for animations.

What is next?

Animation creation, regardless of the software, is an intricate and time-intensive endeavor. Blender, too, is no exception when it comes to the complexities of animation crafting. Every animation-centric project or idea demands dedicated time to meticulously set motion and establish impeccable timing.

One effective strategy for honing your animation acumen is by diving into concise, motion graphics-focused projects. Perhaps a plain texture or a logo gliding onto the screen, enriched with some text, would suffice.

Another avenue worth exploring is fly-through animations driven purely by camera dynamics. Regardless of your project's scale or theme, it's advantageous to curate a select portfolio of animations, enhancing your expertise. To economize on render durations in animation production, lean on Eevee.

Brace yourself for Chapter 8, where we'll delve deeper, furnishing you with nuances of animation production—ranging from content editing and title incorporation to steering objects along preset paths.

Chapter 8 - Animation rendering and composition

In this concluding chapter of our Beginner's Guide to Blender 3.6, we'll delve deeper into advanced animation techniques. A notable aspect we'll explore is how to introduce a "target" to the Blender camera, a feature some might say is "missing."

By utilizing a specific constraint and an Empty, you can establish a target for any camera, assisting in precise framing. This allows the camera to track any object as it maneuvers within the scene.

We will also explore the utilization of 2D curves in animations, particularly beneficial for the "Turntable" animation style. Here, while your objects remain stationary, the camera gracefully orbits around the target. It's an excellent method to showcase 3D models through animation.

Lastly, Blender's remarkable non-linear video editor will be introduced. Here, you'll grasp how to incorporate rendered animations, add text overlays, and integrate swift effects.

Here is a list of what you will learn in this chapter:

– How to make a camera always look to the same object with a Track To constraint

– Make objects follow a path in animation

– Creating animation loops in the Graph Editor

– Render and export video for animation

– Use the Video Sequencer Editor

– Edit, Cut, and compose animations with the Sequencer

– Add backgrounds for animations in the Sequencer

– Add titles for animations using the Sequencer

8.1 Following an object with the camera

Camera framing is an important aspect of any project in Blender for both still images and animations. You might want to use a feature that makes a camera follow an object's motion for animations. That will be useful on several occasions where you have an important subject in animations.

To make your camera follow any object in a scene, use a constraint called *Track To*. Since that constraint is important for animations, it features multiple ways to assign into a 3D model:

- **Using the Constraint tab at the Properties editor**: Select the camera and add the Track To option.

- **Go to the Object → Track → Track To Constraint menu**: Select the camera first and the target object last. Use the menu option to add the constraint.

Both options add a constraint to the camera object that you can edit at the constraint tab (Figure 8.1). You can add the constraint by selecting the camera (1), and after choosing the *Track To* constraint, set the Cube as target (2).

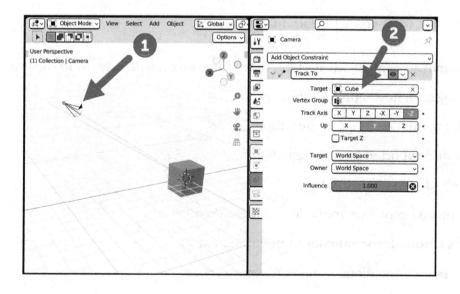

Figure 8.1 - Track To Constratint

A key step in the configuration of this constraint is the target object that your camera will follow, and also the axis used for tracking:

– **To**: Use the -Z option to make your camera look to the object.

– **Up**: Here, you have to use the Y option to align the camera Y-axis with the world Y-axis. Don't change this option unless you want to rotate the camera.

If you use the **Object → Track → Track To Constraint** menu, the target object will be set automatically. For that, you must select the target first and the camera last.

8.1.1 Making an object following a path

Besides making the camera follow an object for animation, we can also use a curve path to help with complex trajectories. If you try to move objects in animation using lots of curves and turns, using a curve object might save time and create a smooth motion.

Using a curve object in Blender, we can make any 3D model use that curve as a path. You can create curve objects using the SHIFT+A keys and go to the Curve group (Figure 8.2).

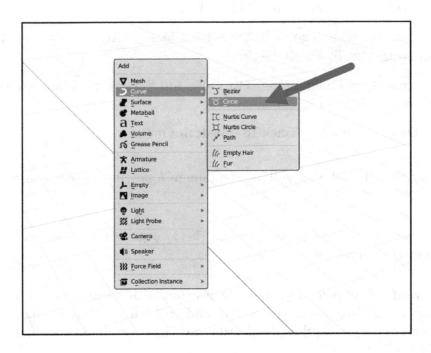

Figure 8.2 - *Curve objects*

From the curve object list, you will see two types of objects:

- **Bezier**: A curve that will feature points control handlers.

- **Circle**: A curve that also has points and control handlers, but already in a circle shape.

Using the Circle option creates a circular shape that can work as a path for animation. If you make the camera follow that circle and use a *Track To constraint*, you will create an animation called "Turntable." In that animation, a camera flies around an object in a circular trajectory.

Assuming you have a 3D model already at the scene. You can follow these steps to create a turntable animation:

1. Create the Circle from the Curve group.

2. Adjust the scale and Z coordinate of your curve with the S and G keys.

3. Select the camera first, and holding the SHIFT key, add the circle to the selection.

4. Press the CTRL+P keys and choose "Follow Path."

5. Select the camera only and got o the **Object → Clear → Origin** menu. That will make the camera origin to align with the circle.

6. Select the camera, and holding the SHIFT key, add the object you want to stay at the center of your circle to the selection.

7. Go to the **Object → Track → Track To Constraint** menu.

If you press the SPACEBAR, you will see the camera following the circle as a path for the animation.

Tip: Use an Empty as the target for your camera. That way you will have more flexibility to move the focus point for your animation.

By default, your follow path animation always start with a length of 100 frames. It uses 100 frames regardless of your settings for Start and End frames. You can change that by selecting the Circle and opening the Object Data tab. There you will find a field called Path Animation (Figure 8.3).

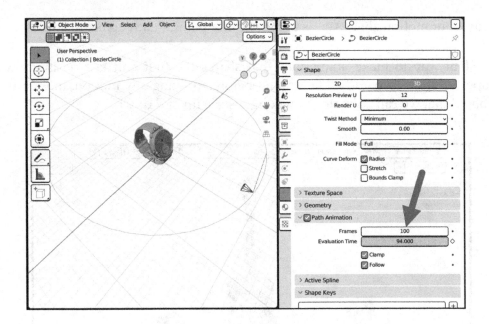

Figure 8.3 - *Path Animation*

Change the Frames option to the amount you want to use for the animation. If you are using the default animation length with an End in frame 250, you can repeat the same value in the Frame field. It will use the entire range of your Timeline.

To break the Follow Path animation, you can select the object following the curve and press ALT+P. Choose the "Clear Parent" option, and the object stops following the curve.

Tip: Be careful not to create a Circle from the Mesh group instead of the Curve. The Circle from the Mesh group doesn't support the Follow Path animation.

8.2 Creating animation loops

Animations in Blender always work in a linear direction, where you define a Start and End frames for them. During playback, the animation begins and ends based on those two frames. However, using a special feature of the Graph Editor, it is possible to make any motion to loop forever or with a defined number of repetitions.

To make an animation loop, you must create the motion first and prepare it to use a loop. For instance, if you want to make an object go back and forward forever, you should work in a way that your last frame uses the same property location value as the first frame.

That way, your motion always ends at the starting point. Ready to begin again!

An excellent way to make animations that shares the first and last positions with the same property values is to add all keyframes before applying any motion. In Figure 8.4, we have an object that we can animate by making it scale up and down.

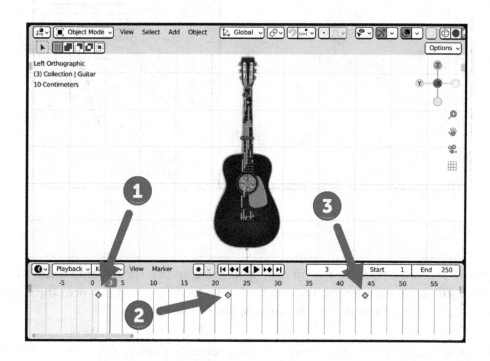

Figure 8.4 - Object for animation with keyframes

The animation will have 1.5 seconds using 30 FPS, which means we need 45 frames. Here is the animation breakdown:

– **Frame 1**: Object will have a scale factor of 1

– **Frame 22**: Object will have a scale factor of 1.5

– **Frame 45**: Object will have a scale factor of 1

Select the object and add a scale keyframe for frames 1, 22, and 45. In Figure 8.4, we have those keyframes highlighted as positions 1, 2, and 3. Since you didn't apply any scale transformation, all keyframes share a scale factor of 1. As an alternative, you can use a SHIFT+D after inserting the first keyframe at the Timeline Editor.

222

Go to frame 22 and apply a scale to the object with a factor of 1.5 by:

1. Pressing the S key

2. Type 1.5

3. Press RETURN to confirm

4. Press I, and add a Scale keyframe to update animation data with the new scale value

Part of the trick of using animation loops is that you should skip the last frame. At the animation settings, make the Start and End frames as 1 and 44. Why not 45 for the End frame?

The reason to use 44 is simple: you want to avoid having two consecutive frames using a scale factor of 1. If you use frame 45 as the End, you will have frames 45, and 1 played in sequence. It will create a brief stop for your animation and break the fluidness of motion.

8.2.1 Using modifiers in the Graph Editor

With the animation ready, we can create the loop by using modifiers in the Graph Editor. Those are different types of modifiers and don't have any relation to modeling modifiers. Open the Graph Editor and press the N key to view the Sidebar.

When we talk about a Sidebar in Blender, you probably think about the 3D Viewport Editor. But, some other Editors also have a Sidebar like:

– Graph Editor

– Dope Sheet

– Shader Editor

– Video Sequence Editor

– Image Editor

For this animation exercise, we have to open a Sidebar for the Graph Editor. Place the mouse cursor above your Graph Editor when pressing the N key to open that Sidebar.

At the Sidebar, open the Modifiers tab (1) and add a Cycles modifier to the curves (2). That creates an animation loop for your selected curves. You will immediately see the difference with the curve visualization extending before and after the original shape (Figure 8.5).

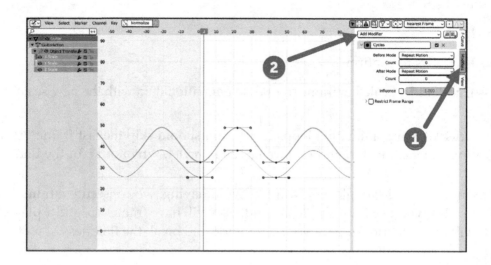

Figure 8.5 - Animation loop with the Graph Editor Sidebar

It is possible to control certain aspects of your loop at the Cycles modifier options. At the Before and After options, you can control the number of repetitions.

Using zero for both, you get the animation repeating forever, or you can pick a number of repetitions to limit your loop. Below you can also restrict the Start and End frames used for the loop. For that, you have the enable *Restrict Frame Range*.

8.3 Organizing projects in scenes

Each project you work in Blender has something called Scene that you can later reference or use for rendering. The scene selector is at the top right of your interface and always start with the default "Scene."

There you can change the current scene and create new ones based on a few options. If you click at the button to the right of your scene name, you will see the types of scenes you can create (Figure 8.6).

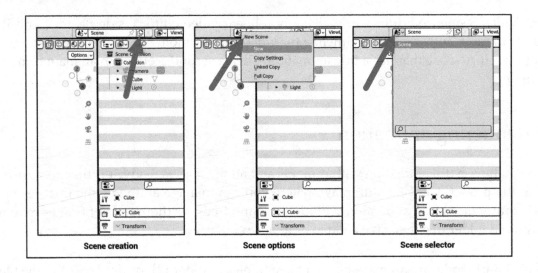

Figure 8.6 - Scene creation, options, and selector

From the options you have:

- **New**: A completely new and independent scene that won't have any objects. An empty new scene.

- **Copy Settings**: An empty new scene that will use some of the settings used from the current scene.

- **Linked copy**: A copy of your current scene that has links to all objects and settings. If you have to create animations with the same objects but using unique types of motion, you can use it.

- **Full copy**: A copy of your current scene with all models and settings but no links with the original objects.

Besides working as a way to organize large projects in Blender, you can also use scenes to render projects in any specific order. If you use the Video Sequencer Editor, it will be possible to instance a full scene for animation editing.

In animation projects, it is common to have multiple takes for the same motion. You can use different scenes to work with shots featuring unique effects and play them in a row at the Video Sequence Editor. Having multiple scenes in a single project makes it easier to use the same assets and 3D models in multiple shots.

The Video Sequence Editor works like a non-linear video editor inside Blender, and it is possible to insert full scenes in a timeline for video composition. For instance, you can have an introductory scene that has a title animation. Then a second scene with all main elements of a project.

8.4 Rendering animation

After you have a full animation with cameras and all the objects ready, it is time to start rendering the project. Unlike a still image where you can manage and view the final result at the Output window, an animation with dozens, hundreds, or thousands of frames requires a dedicated folder to either save a video or image sequence.

Before start rendering animations, you have to pick a folder (2) for the project in the Output tab (1) (Figure 8.7).

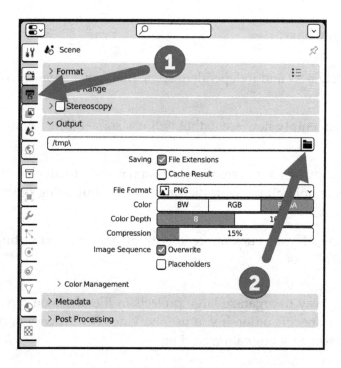

Figure 8.7 - *Output folder*

There you can set a folder in your computer or local network, to save all frames or video from an animation.

Once you have the output folder selected, it is time to make an important choice regarding your rendering. You can save your animation result as a video file or image sequence:

- **Video file**: You can render the animation in formats like MP4, MKV, or OGG

- **Image sequence**: The animation appears as a sequence of individual image files like PNG or JPG.

Having your animation rendered as a video file might be convenient for quick visualization. But if you want to have a flexible workflow and avoid the need for rendering everything again, you should use an image sequence.

The most significant benefit of working with an image sequence is that you can keep a lossless version of all your animation frames. By choosing the PNG image format, you can later generate a video file and include titles and effects.

Another benefit of using image sequences is that you can easily stop and resume a rendering process with no data loss. For instance, by rendering animations with 5000 frames, you can interrupt the process at frame 750. You can later resume the rendering by setting your animation to start from frame 751, which will keep your previous progress.

8.4.1 Rendering as a video file

In case you want to use a video file for the animation output, you have to choose the proper option in the "File Format" field of the Output tab (1). There you will see three main options for the Movie output:

- AVI JPEG

- AVI Raw

- FFmpeg video

Unless you have a very specific reason, avoid using the first two options. If you want to use modern video containers for your animation like MP4, choose the FFmpeg video option (2). With that option, a new panel opens at the bottom of your output settings with a name of Encoding (3) (Figure 8.8).

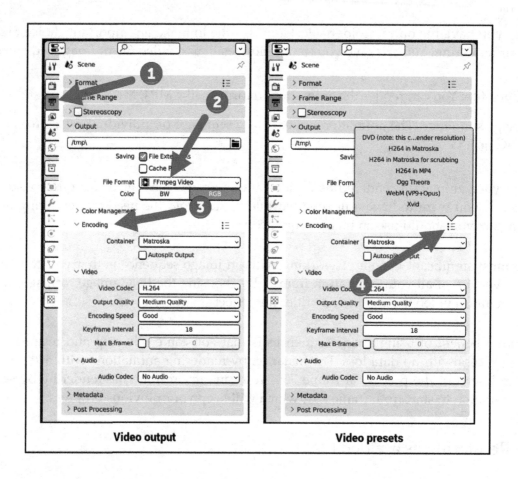

Figure 8.8 - Video output

At the Encoding options, you will choose several options to create an MP4 file or several other formats. For a quick set up in video rendering, you can use existing presets available at the location shown in Figure 8.8 (4).

One of the presets has "H264 in MP4" that already has all the options to create such a file. If you want to render animations for platforms such as YouTube, an MP4 file with h264 is a great choice.

You might want to change a few details about the video to tweak the quality. For instance, change the Output quality from "Medium quality" to "High quality" to get much better quality for animation rendering. Those settings will improve aspects like video bitrate.

That keeps your video file with the highest possible quality and will most likely generate a large file. In the audio field, you will notice that it shows the option "No audio." Because our animation's frames from the 3D Viewport doesn't feature any audio, you should keep the option as "No audio" (Figure 8.9).

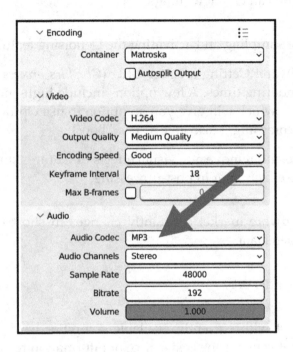

Figure 8.9 - *Audio options*

You can add audio for any animation later in the Video Sequencer Editor and use those settings to control both format and quality for any audio data.

8.4.2 Animation render settings

After choosing where and how to save your animations, it is time to start rendering. You can either press CTRL+F12 or use the **Render → Render Animation** menu. The rendering of animation will most likely take a long time, and you should prepare the computer to stay processing the project for a while.

For projects using Cycles for rendering, processing time might require a couple of hours or days to complete. That depends on a combination of how complex your project is and the available hardware. You can have an idea about how long it will take by making a quick calculation.

If one frame takes on average 1 minute to render and the full length of your animation has 2400 frames, it will take 2400 minutes (1-minute x 2400) to finish. That will roughly give 40 hours of rendering — almost two days of processing the animation.

To reduce that time, you can do a few things:

– Use lower values for sampling and activating the Denoising feature in Cycles;

– Upgrade your hardware! Getting a better GPU (*Graphics processing unit*) might dramatically reduce rendering times. A few options include high-end cards like the RTX family from NVIDIA, which will give you an option to use OptiX Denoising. A better CPU with multiple cores might also give a speed boost.

– Optimize your scene and remove any visual effects or features slowing down the render. Add those same effects later in post-processing.

Since the computer hardware market constantly changes in short periods, I recommend checking the Blender Open Data:

– https://opendata.blender.org/

There you will find a list with currently available computer hardware and their performance for rendering. That is by far the best source of information regarding computer hardware for rendering in Blender.

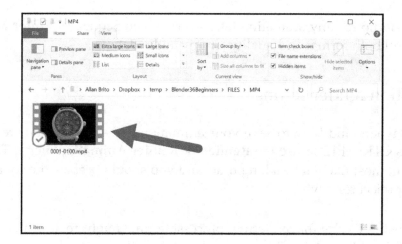

Figure 8.10 - *Video saved in the Output folder*

Once the rendering process comes to an end, you will see the file created in the Output folder (Figure 8.10).

The same applies to an image sequence, but instead of a single file, you will see one image file for each frame.

Tip: A benefit of rendering animations as image sequences is that you can start over the process in case of a problem. For instance, if your computer crashes after rendering frame 1000 from 2400, you can come back and start from frame 1001. In a video file, you would have to start from the beginning.

8.5 Editing and exporting video

The rendering of animation to either a video file or image sequence is the starting point of a process that results in your project's final version. You will most likely use multiple scenes for the animation, effects, and titles. It is possible to edit and add those features in Blender without the need for any external editors.

One of the Editors from Blender can handle and manipulate video files and works like a non-linear video editor. Using the Video Sequencer Editor, or VSE, you can build large animations by manipulating separate pieces of projects like video shots, effects, and more.

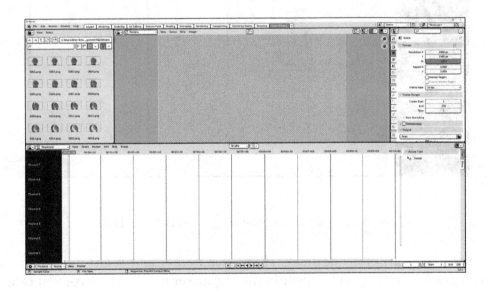

Figure 8.11 - *Video Editing WorkSpace*

To use the VSE, you can use any available space from the interface or open a dedicated Workspace for video editing. The Workspace is the best choice because it already offers all the options to edit and process video comfortably.

From the Workspace selector, you can choose **Video Editing** → **Video Editing** to rearrange the interface with all required spaces to work with video editing (Figure 8.11).

At the bottom, you will see the Video Sequencer Editor with all the channels that can receive tracks such as video, audio, and image sequences. Each channel works like a layer, where you can stack media on top of each other. At the top, you have another Video Sequencer Editor, but with the Preview mode active. That shows a preview of all your media.

In the top right, you have the rendering output settings and a file browser on the left.

You can add content to the editor using the Add menu and choose from video files (Movie), Audio files (Sound), or Image/Sequence (Figure 8.12).

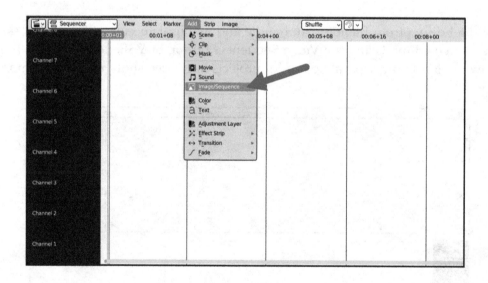

Figure 8.12 - *Add menu from the Video Sequence Editor*

For instance, we can select the Image/Sequence option and select all files from a sequence with the A key. They will appear in the sequencer as a block of content called Strip (Figure 8.13).

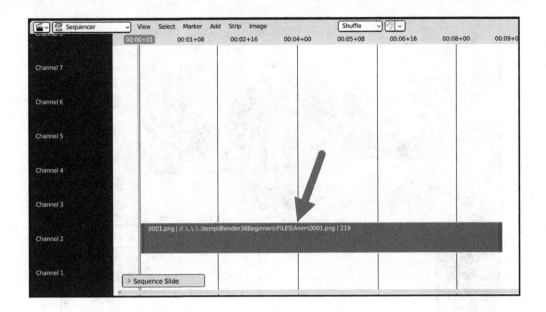

Figure 8.13 - *Image sequence as a track*

To edit and change aspects of any Strip, you can use the same shortcuts applied in 3D modeling tasks. The most used shortcut to manipulate Strips is the G key. Select any Strip and press the G key to move it back and forward in time.

At the borders of the strip, you also find a vertical marker at the beginning and end. You can click to select those markers and using the G key contract or expand the Strip.

If you enabled the transparent option for rendering PNG files as an image sequence, you would be able to compose it with a background easily. Since each channel works as a layer, Strips at the bottom always appear in the back of a composition. Placing a still image at the bottom (1) of your stack makes it appear in the back (Figure 8.14).

To ensure you can see a composition using transparent PNG sequences, make sure you have the Alpha Over (2) option at your Sequencer's Sidebar. By default, a Strip starts with the Alpha Over enabled. Only with that option active, you see transparency applied to Strips (3).

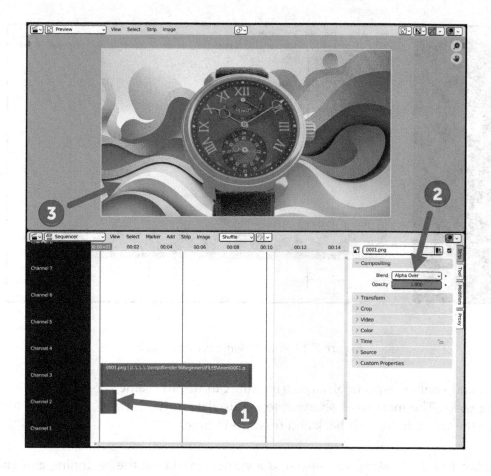

Figure 8.14 - Image in the back

At the bottom, you also have an *Opacity* control a Strip transparency. That is useful in case you need a watermark in a video project.

Tip: You can add keyframes to any property in the Sequencer Sidebar.

8.5.1 Editing video

With the Video Sequencer Editor, you have most of the tools and options from a traditional video editor. For instance, you can cut Strips to remove or reorder parts of your animation. To cut a video, you use the K key with a Strip selected (Figure 8.15).

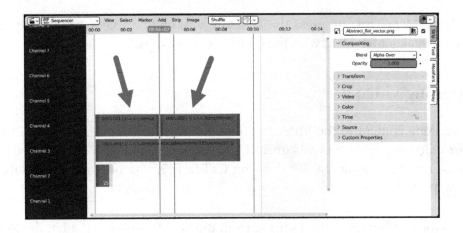

Figure 8.15 - *Cutting a strip*

Place the animation cursor at the frame you wish to cut and press the K key. After you cut a Strip, it will be possible to select each part and:

– Reorder your remaining parts.

– Erase parts of a Strip.

– Duplicate and copy parts of a Strip. You can duplicate Strips with a SHIFT+D.

You can't join two different Strips. Instead, we can make something called a MetaStrip. That is a composed Strip made from several parts. To create a MetaStrip: select multiple Strips and press the CTRL+G keys (Figure 8.16).

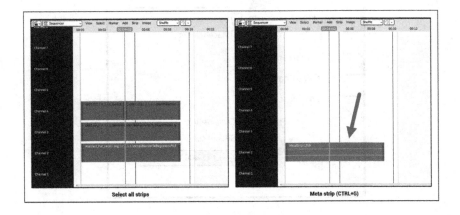

Figure 8.16 - *MetaStrip*

If you select a MetaStrip and press the TAB key, you will be able to edit that group's contents. You can break a MetaStrip with the CTRL+ALT+G keys.

8.5.2 Exporting video

Once you add any content to the Video Sequencer Editor, any rendering from Blender will output your video sequence contents even if you go back to the 3D Viewport and add more content to the original animation. By pressing CTRL+F12, you only see the results of your video editing project.

The reason for that is because of a setting from the Post Processing field at the Render tab. There you will find the "Sequencer" option enabled by default (Figure 8.17).

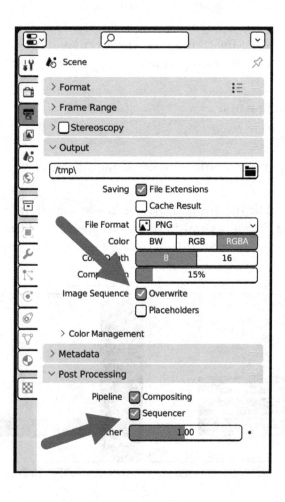

Figure 8.17 - Sequencer option

Unless you disable the Sequencer option, Blender will always output contents from the video sequencer instead of 3D data from your 3D Viewport. If you want to go back to the 3D Scene to change animation aspects, make sure you disable the Sequence option to render it again.

In case you have to edit an existing render, use a different Blender project to edit and cut the animation.

8.5.3 Converting images sequences to video

By adding an image sequence to the Video Sequence Editor, you can convert that to a video file like an MP4. Add the image files as a Strip and change the output settings to use FFmpeg. Pick the settings you need for an MP4 file and start rendering it again.

That is the moment where you can convert an image sequence to a video file, and also add sounds or music. From the Add menu in the Sequencer, you can include Sound strips to the project.

Rendering a video from an image sequence will be much faster than generating all the content from 3D objects. Since you already processed the 3D content, it will be a matter of converting all the effects and images to video.

8.6 Adding titles and text

Most animation projects need some titles in the video to display information before or after the content. That could help you to add credits to the video or a simple title for a project.

To add text to any video in the Sequencer, use the Add menu, and choose the Text option (1) (Figure 8.18).

The text will appear as a separate Strip (2) to edit their contents by selecting the Strip and using the Sidebar (3). You will find options to change details like the font and the text contents (4).

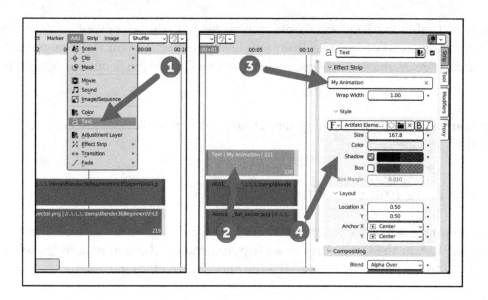

Figure 8.18 - *Text for video*

Add as many text Strips you need for your project, and once you have all the required information for a project, press the CTRL+F12 keys to start rendering your video (Figure 8.19).

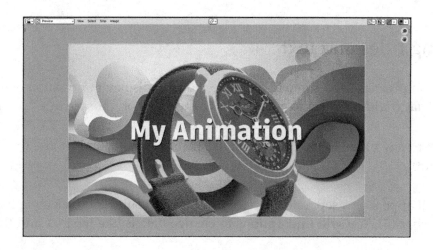

Figure 8.19 - *Titles for an animation*

Remember that your text should be at your sequencer's top channels if you want it appearing on top of any Strips.

What is next?

Having journeyed through this guide, you now possess a strong foundation to embark on various Blender projects, spanning 3D modeling, rendering, and animation. The path ahead? Dream up ideas for visualization and animation projects, and dive right into practice.

As with any new endeavor, the early stages of your projects might present challenges. However, with persistence and the insights from this book, solutions will be within your grasp.

Seize the chance to further refine your Blender expertise. Undertaking personal projects propels you to advanced arenas, such as:

- Character animation

- Advanced rendering

- Visual FX

- Creation of advertisements

- Architectural visualization

- Product design

- Game Development

Blender stands ready to assist in all these ventures. Your task? Concentrate on a specific domain, and you'll steadily gain proficiency in each of these specialized areas.

Figure list

Made in the USA
Monee, IL
25 October 2023

45228190R00136